Praise for

NOT FOR THE FAINT OF HEART

"Sharp and genuine, the book is as much a testament to [Ambassador Sherman's] accomplishments as it is a call to 'find common ground...[and] do good' in an increasingly polarized world. Insightful reading."
—Kirkus

"Wendy doesn't just write about the value of courage, power, and persistence, she lives it. She sees the big picture and sweats the small details, which is why allies and adversaries alike respect her talent and tenacity. She's a living example that a strong negotiator can also be a humane mentor. Her work helped prevent a war and a stop a nuclear arms race. As someone who has been privileged to be Wendy's teammate and even more grateful to remain her friend, I know every reader will learn much from her story but even more from her example."

—John Kerry, 68th Secretary of State and author of *Every Day Is Extra*

"Wendy Sherman draws on childhood lessons of equal justice forged during the civil-rights era to pioneering experiences navigating a professional world dominated by men to illustrate invaluable negotiating skills for women in all aspects of life. Interwoven with revelations about the historic Iran negotiations, hers is a compelling narrative, never needed more than today."

—Andrea Mitchell, Chief Foreign Affairs Correspondent, NBC News Anchor, MSNBC

"A powerful, deeply personal, and absorbing book written by one of America's smartest and most dedicated diplomats. Wendy Sherman gives the reader a vivid, behind-the-scenes account of the historic nuclear negotiations with Iran, capturing essential lessons about the power of human relationships to drive diplomacy. But what truly sets the book apart is how Wendy blends this fascinating account of high-stakes diplomacy with the story of her own incredible life journey. This tale of courage and persistence will inspire readers of all backgrounds, while giving them unparalleled insights into some of the most critical issues of our time."

—Madeleine K. Albright, 64th Secretary of State

"This is an indispensable insider's account of America's negotiations with Iran and North Korea and a timely reminder of the importance of diplomacy. Sherman and her colleagues' struggles to make peace underscore how recently expertise and careful strategy were tangible realities of foreign policy, rather than lost arts. This book is more than that, however. It is also the personal saga of a woman navigating a generation of change in American politics. At an inflection point in our national conversations about diplomacy and gender, this book is illuminating on both fronts."

—Ronan Farrow, contributing writer,
The New Yorker*, author of *War on Peace

"A riveting read. Sherman's candid stories about the way women relate to success, failure, and persistence is a balm for every reader who has been one of a few, or the only woman at the table. This book is a must for anyone who wants to understand what modern, winning talent looks like, and how it can bring two sides together in a world where that is becoming more and more difficult."

—Claire Shipman, journalist and
co-author of *The Confidence Code*

NOT FOR THE FAINT OF HEART

Lessons in Courage, Power & Persistence

AMBASSADOR

WENDY R. SHERMAN

PUBLICAFFAIRS

NEW YORK

PublicAffairs
Hachette Book Group
1290 Avenue of the Americas, New York, NY 10104
www.publicaffairsbooks.com
@Public_Affairs

Printed in the United States of America
First Edition: October 2018

Published by PublicAffairs, an imprint of Perseus Books, LLC, a subsidiary of Hachette Book Group, Inc. The PublicAffairs name and logo is a trademark of the Hachette Book Group.

The publisher is not responsible for websites (or their content) that are not owned by the publisher.

Print book interior design by Jouve.

Library of Congress Cataloging-in-Publication Data has been applied for.

ISBNs: 978-1-56858-816-2 (HC); 978-1-56858-815-5 (ebook);
    978-1-5491-7081-2 (audio)

LSC-H

10 9 8 7 6 5 4 3 2 1

CONTENTS

To the women who came before
To those who lead ahead
To my family with all my love
All that I am and will be, I owe to you.

INTRODUCTION

It was day 25 for me at the Palais Coburg—July 12, 2015. Since the middle of June, inside the white, neoclassical wedding cake of a hotel on Theodor Herzl Platz in Vienna, two exhausted sets of negotiators—one, my team of Americans; the other, from the Islamic Republic of Iran—had been hashing over the last contested passages of the Joint Comprehensive Plan of Action (JCPOA)—more commonly known as the Iran nuclear deal. Its 110 pages, including five complex technical annexes, laid out a path to peaceful resolution of Iran's ambition to have a nuclear weapon.

My team had arrived in Vienna in June to get our feet on the ground before the talks engaged ministers, thinking we'd be home by the Fourth of July. We were now nearly two weeks past our deadline.

The Coburg isn't a bad place for a diplomat to spend a few weeks, it must be said. It lies in the heart of Vienna, where in 1815 the Congress of Vienna—the first real instance of multilateral diplomacy—codified the formal ranks of ambassadors, envoys, and ministers that we still use today. Built in the 1840s as a residence for an Austrian prince, the Coburg has a seemingly endless supply of high-ceilinged meeting rooms adorned with massive portraits of royalty and isolated nooks where, during a break in talks, two adversaries hell-bent on convincing the other can duck in for an impromptu sidebar. The Coburg staff is impeccably discreet (though in a town known as much for its spies as for its diplomats, one never wants to put that discretion to the test). We had plenty of company; the Coburg is popular with Russian oligarchs and their white fur–clad companions as well as with diplomats from around the world coming and going from UN Office Vienna, the sprawling United Nations campus a few miles away across the Danube. The curving, concrete towers of the complex, though taller, are reminiscent of the Watergate, the famous apartments near my office at the State Department, back home in Washington.

The Coburg's staff, its colorful guests, and its proximity to the UN campus weren't the only reasons it was chosen as the meeting place for the final weeks of the Iran nuclear talks. The surrounding roofs overlooking Theodor Herzl Platz provide plenty of vantages for government sharpshooters, making the Coburg a very secure location.

For all its charm and perfectly pitched roofs, the Coburg by day 25 had become a prison. Never mind that I had eaten precisely one meal outside of the hotel in nearly a month, or that I was two weeks past the stay I had packed for. Every available rod and rack in my hotel suite's bathroom was hung with hand-washed laundry.

Out on the square, press from all over the world were huddled at the hotel's entrance, the forest of antennas on the television crews' vans imposing a jarring bit of the modern age on Vienna's old city. Most of the reporters had been there as long as we had, and they could sense in the past few days that the two sides' intensity had picked up, our updates having become vaguer as we edged closer to our final positions. They were counting down to a historic deal to "keep the mullahs from getting the bomb," according to the *New York Times*.

They weren't the only ones waiting. On June 27, US Secretary of State John Kerry, still on crutches from falling off his bicycle in Geneva a month before, had flown in to meet his Iranian counterpart, Foreign Minister Javad Zarif—who himself had just arrived from a quick visit to Tehran, where, it was believed, he'd gotten clearance from the Supreme Leader to finalize the deal.

On their heels came the foreign ministers of the other world powers (known as the P5+1)* who would be involved in the deal—Wang Yi of China, Laurent Fabius of France, Frank-Walter Steinmeier of Germany, Sergey Lavrov of Russia, Philip Hammond of the United Kingdom, and Federica Mogherini of the European Union—all wanting to be on hand in case the end was as close as it looked.

For all the excitement, the agreement was still a tangle of interlocking issues: how to verify Iran's compliance, how to best limit numbers and types of centrifuges, how to "snap back" economic sanctions should Iran fail to live up to the agreement. None of these issues could be solved independently of the others. When one element of the deal was changed, everything else had to be recalculated, and everyone had to be consulted. Then the new information had to be brought to our P5+1 partners and often renegotiated, then back to the Iranians to hash over the same points again. Besides diplomats and technical experts, we had legal opinions from batteries of government lawyers. One session in the final monthlong gauntlet at the Coburg went from early evening until 3:00 a.m. as two sets of lawyers clashed over every word of a single passage.

---

* The United States uses the phrase "P5+1" to describe this negotiation, as defined in this text. The European Union, however, branded the talks the "E3+EU+3," connoting the European countries Great Britain, France, and Germany plus the European Union plus China, Russia, and the United States. The P5+1 label as used in this text is inclusive of the European Union. The coordinating role of the European Union high representative and her team was essential to reaching the agreement.

The best way to describe the negotiation was as the world's most complex and consequential Rubik's Cube. The more you twisted one side to line it up, the more the other sides needed fixing. "No single part of the deal is done until it's all done," I'd tell the press when they asked about what issues were still outstanding. I used the Rubik's Cube comparison so many times, in fact, that one of the technical experts on our team designed his own version, with key phrases from the talks on each colored square. It was such a hit that I had several of them made as keepsakes for members of the team, one of which now sits as an artifact of the negotiation in the Diplomacy Center at the State Department.

When the June 30 deadline passed without a deal, we had extended it. A few more days turned into a week. Then, as one week turned into two, the pressure inside the Coburg cranked higher and higher. The ministers milled around the halls and conference rooms with their squads of aides, unhappy to be stalled here in Vienna, quietly resenting the fact that nothing would be final until Kerry—and President Obama back in DC—said it was, and not quite understanding why we still hadn't reached a deal.

◇◇◇◇◇◇◇◇◇◇

It's not a stretch to say that Vienna, for all its illustrious history as a diplomatic city, had never seen a negotiation quite like this one. Our spell at the Coburg had already broken records—the longest sustained international deliberations, the longest an American secretary of state (or an Iranian one for that matter) had spent in one place. A dialogue that had begun at the United Nations in 2002 as an effort to convince Iran to stop enriching uranium to weapons-grade purity had transmogrified into an entrenched confrontation between the revolutionary government in Tehran and the five permanent members of the UN Security Council (the aforementioned P5), plus Germany (+1). Convened by the high representative of the European Union, the P5+1 talks had become, by the time we reached the Coburg, a de facto bilateral negotiation between Iran and its nemesis, the United States.

Since I joined the talks, after being appointed undersecretary of state for political affairs in 2011, I had led the American team as we wound through Moscow, Baghdad, Istanbul, and Almaty, the remote former capital of Kazakhstan, then back to the traditional diplomatic sites of Geneva, Lausanne, and Vienna. Just before Thanksgiving of 2013, we had arrived at an interim agreement, the Joint Plan of Action, with the expectation that we'd have a final understanding within six months. When six months passed without a conclusion, both sides still held out enough hope that we continued through two more extensions, despite testy disavowals from Tehran and Washington, multiple crises of confidence, raised voices, and, in an unprecedented and completely accidental lapse of diplomatic protocol, a pen sent flying across the table, striking the Iranian lead negotiator.

During this intense time, I had blown past some deadlines of my own. In late May, I had officially announced my retirement from the State Department, effective at the end of the negotiations. At the time, it had seemed reasonable that the talks would wrap up in time for me to accept a fellowship in the fall at Harvard, split between the Kennedy School's Institute of Politics and the Belfer Center for Science and International Affairs. My first study group was slated for shortly after Labor Day. But as the Iran talks dragged on, that start date was tossed out—even if we got a deal, I'd be selling it to Congress until at least the middle of September.

I wasn't the only one on edge. The toll on everyone was enormous. In the weeks since we'd arrived in Vienna, no one had slept much. There were middle-of-the-night video conferences with the White House and "memcons"—memoranda of conversations that we wrote every night describing the day's deliberations for review by the president and cabinet officials. Early morning Vienna time, before the negotiating sessions, we read the intelligence reports that had come in the previous night. Then, all day and into the evening, we sat with our counterparts on the other P5+1 teams, going over every sentence of the agreement and getting prepared for the negotiating sessions with the Iranians themselves.

Apart from the grueling nature of the negotiations, we'd been separated from our loved ones for weeks at a time over the previous years, missing anniversaries, birthdays, and holidays. We'd flown twenty hours to the far side of the globe to achieve very little, endured a sandstorm while trying to get out of Baghdad, improvised meals to fit our religious and food allergy diets, and carried on a poor imitation of our personal lives via smartphone and Skype. We were all ready for life to return to some version of normal.

On July 12, I had arranged to meet the Iranian lead negotiator, Abbas Araghchi, and his partner, Majid Takht-Ravanchi, to discuss the UN resolution laying out the terms of the deal and the limits on ballistic missiles, arms transfers, and other matters that, while not part of the nuclear deal proper, had to be formalized in a resolution that would replace more than a decade's worth of UN resolutions on these same topics. With a new resolution summing up the deal's provisions, the long effort to rein in Iran's nuclear ambitions, which had begun in the Security Council in the early 2000s, would come full circle.

The resolution had always been held out as the last piece of major business precisely because the Security Council partners themselves were not agreed about what exactly it would contain. The United States considered the restrictions on missiles and arms critical. Russia and China, believers in the free transfer of arms and the development of missile technology, didn't want to impose constraints on Iran. Knowing it would be contentious, the partners had arranged to dispose of the resolution only as the rest of the deal was almost ready to be signed. If anyone dug in their heels over these points, they would have to do so when everyone was watching, waiting to go home. That leverage, we figured, would force the parties to find a compromise.

The previous day I had hand-drawn a grid on a ripped piece of notebook paper, laying out the final key elements—the possible limits on missiles and conventional arms, the duration of those limits, and what the sanctions would be for violating them. After dinner on the twenty-fifth day, I met Araghchi and Ravanchi in a private dining room at the Coburg. I put my grid of acceptable formulas in the middle of a small, round table.

As always, Araghchi wore a dark suit with a tieless shirt, in the Iranian style. Fluent in English, an expert in the details of producing nuclear fuel, Araghchi was armed most of all with a steely, determined calm that could be very unnerving to those of us sitting across the table from him. By Araghchi's side, as always, was Ravanchi. Like their boss, Foreign Minister Zarif, the Iranian lead negotiators had been educated in the West—Araghchi in England and Ravanchi at the University of Kansas and in Switzerland. Both had spent their careers in the Iranian foreign service. The difference between them, as we understood it, was that Araghchi had been present in the first days of the Iranian revolution in 1979, when Ayatollah Ruhollah Khomeini had toppled the Shah, and so had the better revolutionary bona fides of the two. Ravanchi, on the other hand, was closer to Zarif, and his opinion was crucial to getting the deal to closure. Equally knowledgeable and equally committed to the revolution, both wore their intransigence like a badge of credibility.

Beside me sat my deputy, Rob Malley, on loan from his position as special White House coordinator for the Middle East, North Africa and Gulf Region. Slight of build and balding on top, Rob is about the sweetest, smartest, most Zen dad I know. He had been a constant and comforting presence since I drafted him a few weeks before from the National Security Council at the White House. Thanks to an upbringing in Paris and his virtually native French, we designated Rob as the "French whisperer," specially assigned to stay close to the French delegation, which was intent on expressing its Gallic independence and would sometimes stray from the agreed-upon script. When trouble loomed, Rob's calm demeanor had always steadied me.

As the meeting got under way, the two Iranians accepted one of the formulations I had set out in my chart. The limits they agreed to would meet the requirements of the president. Suddenly I felt that we were on the verge of success, where only hours before it had felt hopeless.

Then Araghchi sat forward. Before he could attend to the outline of the resolution, he said, there was another point that he wanted to discuss. He began to dispute a point that had been previously settled. This was a regular feature of the Iranian negotiation style: just as consensus seemed imminent, something would suddenly resurface to trouble the waters. *We have given you what you want; now give us something of ours you've taken.*

But at that moment I was out of patience. Too much was at stake as we stood on the precipice of a deal. With all that loomed outside the meeting room door, with the work we'd all done to get to this point, I found this last-minute gambit maddening.

"Abbas, *enough*," I began. "You always want more. Here we are, past the deadline, facing a Congress soon to go on recess..."

I could hear that I had begun to yell, my resentment rising at the Iranians' willingness, at this hour, to play tactical games. And to my frustration, my eyes began to well up with tears. This wasn't the first time this had happened to me, but it was certainly the most inconvenient. I don't know where the wires get crossed in my emotional constitution between fury and weeping. Women learn early in life that it's not socially acceptable to get angry, so maybe my survival instinct throws in another, more disarming emotion to mask my ire. In any case, there was nothing I could do except ignore the tears rolling down my face and push forward. I told the Iranians of my own frustration, how their tactics had completely stalled my own plans. "I have no idea what I will do now, but more importantly, you are risking all we have worked to do."

Araghchi and Ravanchi were stunned. They thought they had learned their way around me, but this weeping, viscerally direct Wendy was a person they hadn't encountered. For the first time in months of tough negotiations, they were in mute disarray. Even Rob sat watching all our faces, not sure how to react.

I would never have planned to push back at Araghchi, or any adversary, with a teary venting session. I could hardly have expected them to take a personal rant as reason to withdraw from their position. But something in the sincerity of my frustration, the realness of the moment, broke through. Everything was at stake in this negotiation, my objection implied—lives that could be consumed in a nuclear battle, yes, but in truth each of our lives and all we had worked for.

After a long silent moment, Araghchi dismissed the objection he had raised. My tears were evidence enough that there was no more give, and we came to agreement on the language for the UN resolution. That tearful reckoning became the final, substantive turn of the Rubik's Cube.

◇◇◇◇◇◇◇◇◇◇◇

Often, when I tell this story at speaking engagements, women come up to me afterward to say that they can relate to my tearful anger. While tears may seem to be a show of weakness—and it's absolutely true that I wouldn't list crying as an essential skill for women operating in the male-dominated diplomatic world—the fact is that when we are ourselves, even if that means letting our tears flow, we can be our most powerful. This is true whether we are negotiating a multilateral nuclear deal, a higher salary at a new job, or an issue in our personal lives. It's true even when facing off against a culture like Iran's, in which women are often treated as subordinates. That day in Vienna proved to me that it's possible for us to be ourselves and still compete in a world that seems often to forbid us from doing so.

That central insight has shaped every lesson I've set out to include in this book. Negotiation cannot be reduced to a set of techniques or strategies that can be applied regardless of the situation or who is negotiating. We have to negotiate with the people in front of us, with their peculiarities, hunches, and particular interests, and we in turn have to bring our authentic selves to how we negotiate. The best negotiators rely not on stratagems or manipulation but on their own experiences. The best skill is to be able to recognize that body of experience and know how to access it and put it to work. This book grew out of the same approach. It tells much more than the story of how I came to negotiate one historic diplomatic agreement. Rather, it frames that story in my particular biography that put me in that position and got me through to success.

We should think of our skill set, in other words, as everything we've done that has formed our sense of judgment—our upbringing, our education, our early achievements, and our mistakes. In diplomacy, as we'll see in the following pages, no time spent on a worthy goal is ever wasted. Life, in its unpredictability, always has something to teach us for the next step, the next job, the next relationship.

This doesn't mean that we shouldn't prepare ourselves for the particular job we want or take necessary steps toward our goals—we should. Indeed, in diplomacy, my colleagues who have expertise in specific regions and areas such as nuclear weapons and arms control are crucial and put in years to acquire such knowledge. We are at our best when we have the practical experience to take the opportunities that come along. But too much focus on hitting career goals can be limiting. When women ask me how I got to do the things I have done, they are often surprised to hear that I had no five-year plan for my life. As a young woman coming of political age during the civil rights movement, the women's movement, and the marches against the Vietnam War, I would have laughed if someone had told me that I would sit opposite Iranians and negotiate a deal about nuclear weapons.

Instead, I got to where I am by rising to fill each role that came my way, including some I didn't expect to do—the head of children's welfare for my home state, the chief of staff to then-congresswoman

Barbara Mikulski, and later Barbara's campaign manager when she ran to become the first Democratic woman elected to the Senate in her own right. After a full career in domestic politics, I turned toward international diplomacy only when I received an out-of-the-blue call to join the State Department. As I grew into my new life as a diplomat, negotiating a missile deal with North Korea and ultimately serving as the first woman undersecretary for political affairs at the State Department, I couldn't have survived on lessons from business books or political science classes. To tell the truth, my best guide was a core set of skills from a master's in social work in community organizing that I had put to work at each turn in my life.

I leaned on my parents' example of courage to act against the expectations of our times. I got to watch other women—colleagues and mentors—own their power and the power their country invested in them. I was exposed to cultures different from mine and learned the value of pulling people of very different backgrounds into a cohesive group. I had to face grave disappointments and circumstances that I couldn't change and find a way to let go and move on. Some of the skills I've needed most I've gained in triumphant, even historic moments. Others I've learned in times of vulnerability, bewilderment, and loss.

I am also aware that I benefited repeatedly from exquisite timing— let's call it luck—and the support of loved ones to make it all possible.

◇◇◇◇◇◇◇◇◇◇

I did eventually get to spend my two months at Harvard's Institute of Politics. The subject of my seminar was "Negotiating Change: How We Took on Some of the World's Toughest Problems and Sometimes Succeeded." Everyone I met at Harvard was interested to know the ins and outs of the Iran negotiation—who said what and how we finally got to yes. More often, however, students and professors alike asked larger questions about how, why, and when any negotiation succeeds or fails. They challenged me to explain why diplomacy is still a useful tool in a world that increasingly seems to respect violence and ultimatums. Most simply asked me how I learned to do what I do. Liberated from the grind of absorbing technical details about uranium enrichment and intelligence reports, I had the chance to reflect deeply on what I'd accomplished and how.

My answers to the young people in my study group were frequently less about diplomatic best practices and more about what I brought to the negotiating table. I found myself explaining things I had always known on some level to be true but hadn't articulated for myself: that the most important facets of the Iran deal were the higher principles we sought and the reimagining of the world that it took to make the deal happen. The deal was the result of our courage in setting it in motion and our persistence in seeing it through. It was anchored by a common wish to make peace and by the common ground we forged with those we negotiated with, and against. We had to use what we had learned about wielding power to change the world and knowing when change is simply not possible. These were all values that I'd grown up with and strengths I've developed along the way. We all have these homegrown skills and qualities, and we can use them throughout our lives, in our careers as well as in attaining our personal goals.

In the dark political era we've entered since I left Harvard, it's increasingly important to know the deeper nature of negotiation. Leaders talk about the art of the deal and discredit the art of diplomacy, while achieving neither and misunderstanding both. Business sense, such as it is, is considered more valuable than political expertise.

The fact is, whether you're in politics or business, the world has now grown so complex that the diplomatic perspective has become indispensable to deal-making.

The contrast that we're facing now in leadership is really between the autocrat and the diplomat. The diplomat weighs things and chooses words and actions carefully; the autocrat acts impulsively (sometimes at 6:00 a.m. on Twitter) without checks and balances. The diplomat is inclusive and expansive, the autocrat transactional and lacking in empathy. The diplomat understands that every decision is grounded in present and past history, with an obligation to the future; the autocrat sees only what's in front of him and what's at stake right now. The diplomat knows that every conversation, every negotiation, every action, is like a move on a giant chessboard that affects all other pieces; the autocrat simply tries to find a way out, the way a child scrawls all over a pizza parlor placemat puzzle with a blunt crayon.

That's the type of leadership that has taken us to where we are now. In May 2018, President Trump pulled the United States out of the Iran deal, a decision that dealt a devastating blow not only to years of diplomacy but to our nation's standing in the world and the world's security. More than that, Trump's decision ignored what long experience taught me: we control only so much in negotiations. Of course we have to be willing to walk away if a deal can't be made, just as we need competence and hard work. But flexing our muscles is hardly the only way to a deal. To make a meaningful deal, we need to see our adversaries not as eternal enemies, or dispensable ones, but as virtual partners. We have to understand the nature of power before we can use it effectively and build a team that can get the job done. And perhaps most of all, we have to persist, to keep fighting for the same ideals that brought the agreement into existence in the first place. That is what this book is about.

chapter one

COURAGE

My father, a residential real estate broker with his own prosperous firm in northwest Baltimore, was attending Rosh Hashanah services at Baltimore Hebrew Congregation, our Reform synagogue on Park Heights Avenue in September 1963. It was a turbulent time for the synagogue, as it was for the country. The month before, Baltimore Hebrew's longtime rabbi, Morris Lieberman, had been one of 200 civil rights protesters—six of them clergymen—to be arrested at Gwynn Oak Park, an amusement park just across the city line that refused entry to African Americans.

For Lieberman, the protest (which resulted in the integration of Gwynn Oak Park a few weeks later) was the latest in a series of civil rights actions he'd been involved in since helping to form the Clergymen's Interfaith Committee on Human Rights a few years earlier. But the rabbi had never been arrested before, and on this High Holiday he went up to the pulpit to explain himself, recognizing that some in the congregation might object to a rabbi who sought out such notoriety.

Lieberman reminded his congregation that as a chaplain in World War II, he had walked through the concentration camps at Dachau after their liberation. Those scenes had made him wonder what the Christian clergy in Germany had done as the Jews were sent away. "What did they preach about on Christmas and Easter in those days?" he wondered. He then put the question to his congregation: could Jews stand by as black citizens of Baltimore were systematically discriminated against? Lieberman cited the Haggadah, the Passover story, which challenges Jews of every generation "to regard himself as though he, in his own person, had been a slave unto Pharaoh." The way to do that in Baltimore in 1963, Lieberman said, was to fight "for the right of those who are still in the slavery of discrimination and degradation."

Deeply moved by the sermon, my father, then not quite forty years old, went to see Lieberman in his office a few days later to ask him what he could do to act on the rabbi's words.

"What do you mean what can you do?" Lieberman responded. "You're a real estate broker. You're more powerful than any priest or any rabbi. You can open up neighborhoods and make it possible for everybody to live wherever they want to live."

Lieberman told my father that if he wanted to take action, he should advertise all of his prospective sales as open housing, available to buyers of any race. That, he said, would make a profound difference.

My father was taken aback. Since moving his family to Maryland fifteen years before, he had managed to build his thriving real estate office, Mal Sherman Inc., in part by selling houses to black families who were moving out of the city's minority neighborhoods, which were full to bursting in the booming postwar years. After finding them homes in our old Jewish neighborhood, Dad would then sell new homes further north to the white families who had sold their homes to the black families.

The unwritten rules of the African American migration into new neighborhoods were strict, however. Any broker who sold a house in a white part of town to a minority courted animosity. Brokers who introduced African Americans to a street with the intention of panicking white families and flipping their houses were liable to be accused of "blockbusting."

"If I do this," my father told Rabbi Lieberman, "I'll be run out of town."

"Well, you asked what you could do," the rabbi responded.

My father went home to talk with my mother. Though she too saw that it spelled financial ruin for them, my mother agreed that they needed to follow Lieberman's call. Some of my father's real estate colleagues counseled patience. The civil rights demonstrations like the one at Gwynn Oak Park were slowly turning the tide. Some activists were already agitating for open housing laws. Legislation would eventually come, and he would be better protected then, his friends told him.

But Dad was determined. The following month my father announced that Mal Sherman Inc. would, as company policy, sell to all individuals, regardless of race, creed, or color, as long as his agents could find an owner who would sell. Within six months, he had lost more than 60 percent of his listings.

It was not, to his surprise, our neighbors who stopped giving him their houses to sell—it was his competition, the dozen and more brokers whom he was beating month in and month out. "The brokers in the area proceeded to tell the marketplace that they ought not to do business with us," Dad explained at a hearing of the US Commission on Civil Rights some years later. Home builders who had given Mal Sherman Inc. hundreds of listings in the real estate boom time stopped calling. Those in the industry who did call were phoning in their displeasure. I vividly remember picking up the phone at our house and hearing threats laced with racial epithets. In a time when riots were breaking out and bombs were going off all over the country, their angry threats to bomb our house seemed very real.

For a time, Dad was able to make up much of the lost revenue from referrals he got from civil rights groups. The local Congress of Racial Equality chapter and the NAACP sent him business, as did Baltimore Neighborhoods, an organization working to improve housing prospects for African Americans in the city. Some individual white homeowners called him offering to sell their homes to black buyers.

Soon his reputation for providing good homes for black families caught the attention of the local professional sports teams, all of whom asked him to find housing for their black stars. In the winter of 1966, the Cincinnati Reds traded Frank Robinson to the Baltimore Orioles. After learning that he was going to be moving to town, Robinson called my father. "I'm coming to play baseball for the Orioles this year," Robinson told him. "We want to live in an all-white or mixed neighborhood. We want good schools and a safe neighborhood." The only house Dad could find for Robinson that first year was in Ashburton, a relatively well-to-do but all-black neighborhood in northwest Baltimore.

That summer the Orioles won the World Series, and Robinson was named Most Valuable Player. The following spring, Robinson informed Frank Cashen, the general manager of the Orioles, that he would not come to training camp unless his family could live in an integrated neighborhood as he'd requested. Cashen called my father from Florida, yelling that he had to find a house for Robinson. My father finally found a suitable rental, after promising the neighbors signed baseballs and bats. Even at that, the owner of the house upped the rent to $500 a month, from $300.

My father's business couldn't survive on these special accommodations, however. He turned to land sales and insurance to make up what he had lost, but by 1968 his office had closed. We had already given up our spacious house in a Baltimore suburb for a smaller one in a less affluent neighborhood. But my parents never questioned their choice. Real change, they knew, almost always comes at a price.

◇◇◇◇◇◇◇◇◇◇

I've often wondered what gave my father and mother the courage to fight discrimination, knowing how much it would cost them. Nothing in Dad's fractured early life provides many clues. His father, a wealthy Philadelphian named Abraham Silverman, committed suicide when Dad was only five years old. His mother reacted to her husband's death by starting over, even changing the family name from Silverman to Sherman. She lived the high life in Manhattan and Paris. (My grandfather's million-dollar life insurance policy did not exclude suicide.) She shipped my father and his older sister off to a Catholic boarding school in Lausanne, Switzerland. He returned when he was ten, finished high school at Horace Mann, a private high school in the Bronx, and after a year-plus at the University of North Carolina, enlisted in the Marines after Pearl Harbor.

Spirituality was certainly part of what inspired him. My father had come to Judaism late in life. He had been spurred to explore his faith by his marriage to my mother, Miriam, but he only really embraced it after the death of his sister, who, like their father, killed herself before reaching midlife. He came to regard Rabbi Lieberman, more than a decade older than he, as a father figure. Never having been bar mitzvahed, my father never felt fully accepted as a Jew. Nevertheless, he found serenity in the rituals of prayer, and I cherished sitting all day with him in High Holiday services.

Yet that wasn't the whole answer. His conversion to civil rights activism had begun long before he met with Lieberman. As early as 1953, ten years before Lieberman issued his challenge, my father had fought the practice of blockbusting by trying to convince our white neighbors to accept his black clients. In 1960, he integrated his office, hiring a black agent, Lee Martin, straight out of nearby Morgan State University—tellingly, he was the only agent at the time who had a college education—and paying him $100 a week for six months until he could generate his own clients.

Though many factors contributed to my father's extraordinary courage, I think that it was seeing combat that gave him his ideas about social justice. At the outbreak of the war, he enlisted in the Marines, no doubt a jarring change from his Swiss boarding school upbringing. He was sent to the Pacific, where he fought, and was wounded, in the Guadalcanal Campaign. He never spoke much about what had happened in the war—so few veterans did—but when he came back in 1945, he was dedicated to the cause of peace. When he was still an enlisted Marine, he was active in the founding of the American Veterans Committee, a liberal (and racially integrated) answer to the American Foreign Legion. With my mother, he attended the opening meetings of the United Nations in San Francisco as a delegate from the United Nations Veterans League, which he'd helped form, arguing that any organization that worked for peace needed to hear from those who had fought.

My father was hardly the only person to be radicalized for peace by the experience of war. John Kerry, my future boss at the State Department, was another. A lower-middle-class kid from Massachusetts, Kerry was sent to a tony New Hampshire boarding school by an aunt, then went on to Yale. After enlisting in the US Navy, he volunteered for the Swift Boat team that would take him into combat in Vietnam. He came out of the war dedicated to a life of service and the pursuit of peace. The first time John Kerry was in a Senate hearing room was when he testified, wearing his military fatigues, before the Foreign Relations Committee about the protests of his group, Vietnam Veterans Against the War, with Senator William Fulbright providing the questions. Kerry challenged the committee to think about war, not in terms of patriotic abstractions, but in terms of the people on the ground. "Each day, to facilitate the process by which the United States washes her hands of Vietnam," the young Lieutenant Kerry said, "someone has to give up his life so that the United States doesn't have to admit something that the entire world already knows, so that we can't say that we have made a mistake.... We are asking Americans to think about that because how do you ask a man to be the last man to die in Vietnam? How do you ask a man to be the last man to die for a mistake?"

I believe my father would have chosen a similar course if he'd been of Kerry's generation—that he would have elevated his activism to a campaign for elected office where he could do the most good. But my father lived through a different war and a different homecoming. Like many of his fellow World War II vets, my father yearned for a normal life of family and work. He chose the life of a salesman. In San Francisco, where he had recovered from his war wounds, he took a sales job with the California vintner Paul Masson. When my parents, with my sister in their arms and me on the way, moved to

Maryland in 1949 to be closer to my mother's family, my father asked his uncle, a successful stockbroker, which field he thought my father should go into. Seeing all the GIs returning from the war, his uncle suggested that he sell either insurance or real estate.

My father was wonderfully suited to finding people homes. He was warm, with a wide smile under expressive eyes, and he was partial to colorful bow ties—the MAL SHERMAN REALTOR sign outside his office in Baltimore was in the shape of a formal white bow. At its peak in the mid-1950s, the office employed as many as twenty busy agents as Baltimore's suburban areas boomed.

But my father's true talent as a salesman was his ability to imagine possibilities—to see a house's potential as a home, or a new development's promise as a real neighborhood. That same imagination allowed him to see the world as other than it was, and how it could be better, more equal, more fair. That is what drove him to change his corner of Baltimore, and through it, the world. He and my mother taught me that when we're faced with adversity and stubborn history, having the courage to stick to our vision can see us through to a good and right end.

My father saw the possibilities in his children as well. "You could be the first woman senator from the state of Maryland," he used to say to me when I was young. I've realized that the life of service and policymaking he envisioned for me was really the one he had imagined for himself.

If he passed his dreams down to his children, he made sure to also pass along his courage—not by lecturing us but by example. When I was about fifteen, my father took me along to an appearance by Lena Horne at Coppin State College, a historically black college in Baltimore. Horne hadn't come to Coppin State to perform. A decade earlier, during the McCarthy era, the singer and actress had been blacklisted by the major movie studios for her ties to Paul Robeson and other Communist Party members. By the time my father and I went to see her, she'd fought her way back into Hollywood's good graces, but the studios hadn't succeeded in quieting her support for civil rights or her protests against the industry's legacy of discrimination.

My father and I squeezed into a crowded meeting room. The mood was electric, and to me frightening. We were the only white people in the room, or so it seemed to me then. Sheltered in my white, Jewish community, I had never felt what it meant to be the outsider, the "other." Yes, I was Jewish, and once, on a cross-country driving trip, my family had been told that no rooms were available at a hotel where there were clearly some vacancies, but we kids hardly noticed. I considered myself part of America's white majority, one of those whose behavior was at issue that night.

As disorienting as it was, that evening introduced me to something big and visceral and strange. I could feel how a person who is ready to take on the challenge could be swept up by the fight for what's right, for a better future. My father had a passion for justice that was rebellious, even a bit reckless. Beneath the real estate salesman's dapper, reassuring exterior, Dad harbored a single-minded will to change what he saw around him and to connect with those who thought the same way. He had felt a kinship his whole life with those who spoke out or stood up for what was right. He had needed Rabbi Lieberman to give him license, to vault him into a life where he would risk much and ignore the economic costs of following his beliefs. This sense of civic or even religious duty can't be instilled in a person by reading or thinking. It's something that happens to you. Dad was trying to spark it in me.

I've never been the reckless type. As a kid, I devoured biographies of great women leaders like Joan of Arc, Harriet Tubman, and Florence Nightingale, and I even drew inspiration from Nancy Drew, the fictional girl detective. Looking back, what impressed me about these women was that they wouldn't be deterred. Similarly, my father's courage comes out in me in a very directed, disciplined form. My brand of courage lies in being able to back up my vision with discrete goals and drive myself toward them, inspiring others to follow me.

Men and women of character find their courage in the times they live in. Dad found it in the civil rights struggle in Baltimore. Barack Obama found his way into public service after serving as a community organizer in Chicago. Barbara Mikulski, another community organizer, brought African Americans and white working-class citizens together to stop a six-lane highway from destroying their east Baltimore neighborhoods. From there she garnered a seat on the city council and ultimately was elected a US senator. My times, I thought, demanded someone different who could block out the noise of detractors and doubters and make a deal that few had the courage to imagine could actually happen. I keep everyone focused on the possibility of getting to success. What I took from my father's courage was the fortitude to get through the darkest hour—to make it to the end of a trying week, whether beset by crisis or suffering the most mundane tedium, knowing sometimes the best one can do is to make it to the end of the day.

◇◇◇◇◇◇◇◇◇◇◇

In politics, as in our personal lives, what often takes the most courage is to change a relationship that is frozen, damaged by past events. Both parties may want to reconcile, but neither is able to take the first step. To open yourself to reconciliation is to be vulnerable. The recent history of relations between the United States and Cuba is a good case study of how to change a frozen relationship.

In early 1993, I joined the State Department for the first time as assistant secretary of state for legislative affairs. Working under Secretary of State Warren Christopher, I represented the State Department on Capitol Hill, pushing the administration's agenda in front of the foreign relations committees and defending our budgets to Appropriations.

Not long after I started, what had been a simmering problem of Cuban refugees crossing to Florida in rickety rafts came to a head: by July 1994, what had been a trickle of émigrés—a few hundred a year—had steadily grown to a constant stream of some five hundred rafters a month. In August, Fidel Castro, who saw the outflow as a way to put pressure on the United States for its decades-long trade embargo, announced that he would no longer make any move to stop people from leaving. Suddenly more than thirty-five thousand Cubans were headed for Miami's beaches from all over Cuba, and the US Coast Guard was left to avert a humanitarian disaster on its own.

Most of those plucked out of the sea were being held at Guantánamo on the southern coast of Cuba, then a US Marine base, not the infamous prison it would become after 9/11. There, thousands awaited asylum decisions. Out in the Florida Straits, meanwhile, boats were sinking. People were dying. In the spring of 1995, Senator Bob Graham of Florida visited Guantánamo and on his return went to the Oval Office to warn President Bill Clinton that the overcrowded facilities there were about to boil over.

President Clinton had come into office wanting to find a way to move our Cuba policy forward. The trade embargo, when first instituted by a series of executive orders in the early 1960s, was designed to pressure the young Castro government to compensate business owners for the companies he'd nationalized since coming to power and to urge the regime toward democracy. Fifty years later, Cuba showed no sign of complying, nor had depriving the Cuban people of access to the American economy caused the Castro regime to blink, much less fail. For most of its tenure, the embargo had only justified Fidel Castro's continuing dictatorship, passed off as a revolutionary stance with the United States in the role of imperialist aggressor. "Anybody with half a brain could tell the embargo was counterproductive," President Clinton told historian Taylor Branch in the fall of 1995 in an interview that appeared in Branch's book *The Clinton Tapes*.

To the president, the refugee crisis represented an opportunity to work with the Cubans to coordinate our responses and perhaps a chance at a wider dialogue. In the short term, improved relations could give poor Cubans fewer reasons to abandon their homes to head for American shores. In the long run, it could lead to broader diplomatic discussions with the government.

It's difficult at this remove to appreciate how much political courage it took for President Clinton to reach out to Castro. Shaking up a long-standing policy, even an unproductive one, always makes the public uneasy, but any effort at relaxing tensions with the Castro regime was guaranteed to anger Cuban Americans in particular. These were the people whose families' property Castro had expropriated in the revolution, and they were deeply committed to a full-on embargo. They were also extremely powerful as voting blocs in south Florida and New Jersey.

The sensitivity of the Cuban community is an example of why a president normally saves foreign policy shake-ups for the second term, when he (or someday she) no longer risks paying a penalty at the voting booth. At the time President Clinton began his initiative, he had been president for less than half of his first term.

Nevertheless, Clinton quietly opened negotiations with Cuba, sending a top State Department official to meet with a member of Castro's Kitchen Cabinet, first in New York and later in a bar in Toronto. A month later, in May 1995, the president announced the fruits of the talks. As a concession, the United States would no longer grant automatic asylum to refugees from Cuba. Those at Guantánamo would be admitted over a period of three months, but any future refugees would be dealt with according to what became known as the "wet foot/dry foot" policy—if they were caught at sea, the Coast Guard would usher them back to Cuba; those who were able to make landfall on US territory would be allowed to stay.

Republicans in Congress responded quickly and harshly, showing exactly why upsetting the status quo requires courage. "It's time to tighten the screws," declared Senator Jesse Helms, a North Carolina Republican. With Indiana representative Dan Burton, Helms proposed a bill that would reinforce the embargo. For the first time, countries besides the United States and Cuba would be pushed to comply with our embargo, as Helms-Burton would put sanctions on any company, even a foreign one, that did business with Cuban firms.

As the State Department's representative on the Hill, I spent that fall arguing that the Helms-Burton bill was a bad idea. It wasn't a difficult argument. As a purely political gesture, it would backfire, since it would call more attention to a policy that was being blamed for deaths at sea. Substantively, it would be worse, rankling our friends abroad. For instance, we would be required to penalize Canada for its centuries-long habit of buying Cuban sugar.

Helms-Burton passed the Senate but failed to gain traction in the House. We had won the round.

Four months later, the president's fledgling Cuba policy was shot down out of a blue sky. Since 1991, an organization called Brothers to the Rescue had been flying over the Florida Straits to search for refugees afloat. When they spotted a raft, the Brothers pilots would alert the Coast Guard to the boat's whereabouts. The Brothers had other concerns besides the refugees' safety: their flights were directly aimed at promoting the flow of Cubans to Guantánamo and the States.

Emboldened by the heightened air of crisis and Clinton's outreach to Cuba, the Brothers expanded their missions and began to stray into the airspace over Havana. When they met no resistance, they returned to drop leaflets advocating further ties with the United States. The Cuban government registered its complaints each time, but the White House seemed powerless to stop the overflights.

In February 1996, a Cuban MIG-29 shot down two of the Brothers' Cessnas. Clinton's diplomatic effort was at an end. The president had no choice but to demand a UN resolution condemning what the Cubans had done. He tightened restrictions on flights to Cuba and hemmed in Cuba's diplomats in New York.

To say that Helms-Burton was suddenly reborn is an understatement. When news of the shoot-down broke in Washington, I happened to be at a routine hearing before the House Foreign Affairs Committee. In almost real time, I went from arguing against the need for the legislation to accepting it as a fait accompli.

Given the advantage, Congress added a twist to the knife. The embargo, which for fifty years had been primarily left to the White House to plan and execute, would now be enshrined in Helms-Burton as law, giving Congress unprecedented control. We tried to argue that this amendment would interfere with the president's constitutional right to run the country's foreign affairs, but the fix was in. Helms-Burton was now the law of the land.

The Cuban refugee crisis would have one more chapter, written five years after Helms-Burton went into effect. It would only exacerbate tensions over the plight of the Cubans.

In November 1999, a six-year-old boy named Elián González was found floating in an inner tube off the coast of Florida. He and his mother had been on their way from Cuba when their aluminum boat sank. Elián's mother and ten others had drowned. Under normal circumstances, the boy, not having reached land, would have been returned to Cuba, where his father still lived. Elián had the further bad luck, however, to become stranded over Thanksgiving weekend. When the Coast Guard picked up the boy and, following protocol, put in a call to a State Department duty officer to start the process of returning him, nobody picked up the phone immediately.

A few months before, my friend Madeleine Albright, who had been named secretary of state in Clinton's second term, had asked me to return to State as her counselor. As part of that portfolio, she had assigned me to pick up the quiet but well-established channel to the Cuban government.

Thanksgiving is my favorite holiday, and as often as I could I played host at my house in the Washington suburbs. Traditionally, family arrived on Wednesday night to bake pies. Thursday morning I'd get up early to make stuffing, prepare the turkey, and get it in the oven. Friday was an outing for the women to a local clothing outlet and meals of leftovers.

Amid this delicious chaos, my phone rang. It was the State Department operations center, calling to tell me that a young Cuban had been brought into Florida, his mother having drowned at sea. I quickly put a conference call together of all relevant actors, from the Coast Guard to the assistant secretary for Western Hemisphere affairs to immigration authorities.

But it was too late. Elián was already on land, and under the wet foot/dry foot policy, he had the right to stay. The boy was quickly turned into a political football. Elián's father back in Havana wanted him home, but his émigré relatives in Miami—led by his paternal great-uncle, who had been expecting him and his mother—did not want him returned to the Communist nation. Many Cuban Americans were in an uproar, insisting that democracy, not communism, was best for Elián.

The arguments and court reviews went on for months, involving Attorney General Janet Reno; Elián's uncle, a US resident who took custody of the poor kid; his two Cuban grandmothers, who came to the United States to plead for his return; and a federal judge, who granted a stay while Elián's relatives applied for asylum. In the end, Reno decided that Elián should go home, and federal agents in camouflage were photographed storming the Miami home of his relatives. Shortly afterward, another court proceeding determined that he was too young to apply for asylum himself, and his father was unwilling to apply on his behalf. On June 28, 2000, more than seven months after his boat sank, Elián left for Havana. US-Cuban relations were frozen again.

At a key point in the six months of Elián's travails, I spoke with Ricardo Alarcón, the head of Cuba's National Assembly and part of the country's senior leadership. Alarcón and I had met just once, for a get-acquainted meeting in a restaurant near the East River in New York—Cuban officials could only enter the United States for United Nations functions, and then they had to stay within twenty-five miles of the UN headquarters. That day we talked about the US-Cuba relationship and what the future might hold, and Alarcón gave me his personal phone number. I never thought I would have occasion to use it.

President Clinton could have at any point made political hay with the Cuban exile community by publicly urging asylum for Elián, although the decision rested with the Department of Justice and the courts. But undoubtedly influenced by First Lady Hillary Clinton, a longtime children's advocate, the president courageously affirmed that it would be in the "best interests of the child" to be returned home. I knew that the president was right—if Elián and his father had been in America, his return would have been an open-and-shut case.

◇◇◇◇◇◇◇◇◇◇◇◇

It might be surmised from the history of President Clinton's Cuba policy that courage is never rewarded in politics, but it's more complicated than that. The lesson is the same one my father learned when trying to integrate Baltimore neighborhoods: one courageous gesture is rarely enough. Having begun to make a change, we are usually rewarded by being asked to take further risks until the job is done.

When President Barack Obama came into office, he also looked for a window to change Cuba policy, but with the Great Recession and his ambitious health-care bill to deal with, he knew it would have to wait for a second term.

Soon after his second inaugural, Obama set his own secret talks in motion. Obama asked his deputy national security adviser, Ben Rhodes, and the National Security Council's Latin American director, Ricardo Zuniga, who had served in the US interest section in Havana, to conduct the talks, which would be held in Canada. Obama believed that it was important to signal to the Cubans that the plan had close presidential support, so he kept the negotiations privy to only a very small group of White House staff, much to the dismay of the State Department.

Originally, the focus of discussion was on Alan Gross, an American who had been held in a Cuban military prison for five years. Gross had gone to Cuba as a contractor for the US Agency for International Development (USAID), an agency that promotes development around the globe. Gross's planned project was to help get members of the Jewish community in Cuba online, and he had brought with him several servers and other computer equipment. The Cubans had accused him of being a spy.

Just sixty years old at the start of his ordeal, Gross looked much older than sixty-five by the time Obama sent Rhodes and Zuniga to meet with the Cubans. He had shed a scary amount of weight in hunger strikes protesting his detainment, and illness had cost him some of his teeth. Over the years of his detention, Judy Gross, Alan's indomitable wife, tried to be understanding about the limits of what his government could do, but meetings with her were extremely wrenching. How do you not cry, and even rage, when your husband is not there for weddings or illness or graduations, let alone daily life?

When the talks began in Ottawa in the summer of 2013, the Cubans surprised Obama's emissaries by wanting to discuss more than Alan Gross. They expanded the topics on the table to include their entire diplomatic relationship with the United States. This unexpected opening asked the president to take a much bigger risk than making a swap for a US contractor who had been accused of being a spy. A narrow deal to free Alan Gross would be roundly applauded at home; a broader deal would not only bring the usual objections from the Cuban community but tie Obama to a regime in whom we Americans had little trust. Egged on by the pope, who hosted a round of talks in Rome, and with support from some courageous members of Congress, the discussions continued for eighteen months. In December 2014, President Obama announced that Alan Gross was coming home, and named Roberta Jacobson at State as Assistant Secretary for Western Hemisphere Affairs to negotiate the normalization of diplomatic relations with Cuba.

The embargo would remain in effect, but commercial flights were regularized, travel was made easier, and remittances back to families in Cuba were allowed to increase. An embassy was opened in both capitals, and trade was increased. Obama's words said it all: "Change is hard, in our own lives and in the lives of nations, and change is even harder when we carry the heavy weight of history on our shoulders. But today, we are making these changes because it is the right thing to do."

◇◇◇◇◇◇◇◇◇◇

Perhaps no relationship with any country has been as frozen as that between the United States and Iran, and our leaders have struggled for decades with even deciding whether to find the right path forward.

Many Americans first became conscious of Iran when supporters of the Muslim cleric Ayatollah Ruhollah Khomeini overthrew the Shah of Iran. In November 1979, a group of Iranian university students, devout followers of Khomeini, occupied the US embassy in Tehran, taking fifty-two Americans hostage.

The embassy's occupiers objected to our country's long support for the Shah of Iran, who had modernized Iran's economy in the 1950s and '60s and secularized its Islamic culture, but who had also ruled with an iron fist. To these radical students, the United States was not an ally but a colonial power, one that had helped Great Britain regain control of the Iranian oil fields in 1953 by engineering a coup against the Iranian prime minister Mohammad Mossadegh, who had threatened to nationalize them. For the next year and seventy-nine days, Americans raptly followed the fate of the embassy personnel—the long-running ABC news program *Nightline* began as a nightly update on the crisis. As a turning point in American awareness of and opinion about the Middle East, the Iran hostage crisis is outdone only by the 9/11 attacks. When President Jimmy Carter's attempt to free the hostages with a military rescue mission failed, it seemed to expose America's post-Vietnam impotence and helped decide the 1980 presidential election, in which Jimmy Carter lost to Ronald Reagan.

The revolution also caught our attention at the gas pump. Iranian oil production slowed during the revolution, sending gasoline prices soaring and creating lines at gas stations reminiscent of the oil shortages suffered five years earlier. In retaliation, President Carter declared an embargo on Iranian oil. We froze Iranian bank accounts and, under Reagan, stopped trade with Iran altogether.

Ever since, the mistrust between the United States and Iran has been profound. Our two embassies tell the tale. The Shah's opulent Modernist embassy on Massachusetts Avenue in DC, once the site of swanky parties, is in mothballs. Outside the American embassy in Tehran, a tourist site, hangs a banner reading DEATH TO AMERICA.

Today's Iranian leaders were born into politics during the revolution. Those days stunned the world—and probably the participants themselves, who could never have expected such a far-reaching impact. That experience is still the glue that holds the Iranian ascendancy together, like a shared experience of combat, college, and an industry-disrupting start-up rolled into one. The centerpiece of this powerful bonding experience, of course, is the taking of the American embassy. The United States is the "Great Satan," the enemy of the revolution, but we also represent the revolution's greatest success.

This revolutionary posture is crucial to understanding the progress of the Iran deal. Official Iran maintains a kind of split personality. On the one hand, the Supreme Leader and the elected government sit atop one of the most enviably stable societies in the Middle East, with a broad and literate middle class. They have been the ruling elite for a generation. The Islamic Republic of Iran has for years unrepentantly projected its power across the Middle East. They support the Lebanese terrorist group Hezbollah in its campaigns against Israel and back Shi'ite fighters in Iraq. More recently, Iran has sent arms to antigovernment rebels in Yemen and helped President Bashar Al-Assad brutally put down a rebellion in Syria. Iran's activities have also led it into a power struggle with Saudi Arabia that is increasingly viewed, not only as a political fight, but as a contest between the Sunni and Shi'a branches of Islam.

On the other hand, Iran's leaders still consider themselves besieged by an anti-Muslim West, led by the United States, that is obsessed with their overthrow. At times our domestic politics can play into their script; for the most part, however, we oppose their machinations for reasons of national security and to protect our allies. Either way, the Iranian political and religious ascendancy relies on demonizing the United States as a way of making themselves look heroic and necessary.

The politics of Iran is by no means monolithic. The Islamic Revolutionary Guard Corps (IRGC) is a powerful, nearly autonomous military organization of some 125,000 that protects the values of the revolution, but there are also conservatives and liberal reformers, intellectuals and populists, though in our terms we might call them hard hard-liners and hard-liners.

The psychology of Iran's factions can sometimes flummox the most seasoned diplomats. I got my education in the roiling forces inside Iran in my first month as "P"—as the undersecretary for political affairs is known in the halls at State—in September 2011. I'd spent my first week at the opening of the United Nations General Assembly session, the annual ingathering of delegates also attended by heads of state to address the body and hundreds of visiting ministers. I introduced myself around to my new counterparts and joined Secretary Hillary Clinton for the frantic schedule of meetings and impromptu huddles—known in the trade as diplomatic "speed dating"—that take place during the General Assembly.

It wasn't until a week later that I got back to DC and was able to move into my office on the seventh floor of the State Department building. The seventh is the power floor, synonymous with the top officials—the secretary ("S"), the deputy secretary of state ("D"), the deputy for management and resources ("DMR"), the undersecretary of state for political affairs, and all their staffs. What is known as Mahogany Row—a gallery hung with portraits of the previous secretaries of state—connects the offices so that the occupants of these offices can visit each other privately without coming or going through the reception area.

At some point, I went in to see Deputy Secretary Bill Burns, who had been handling Iran matters when he was "P," and asked whether he wanted to keep the portfolio. "It's all yours," Burns said, with seeming satisfaction. Neither one of us realized at that moment that Bill had set me off on an adventure that would consume the bulk of my time and attention (not to mention air miles) for the next four years—or that soon enough, Iran would draw him back in as well.

We don't always get to pick the chapters in our lives that will test us, and often the most courage is required in jumping into a situation with no expectation of changing it, much less adequate preparation. I had little expertise in Iran and certainly no affection for the place. I never thought I'd develop the intimate acquaintance I now have with the country's intense, internecine politics. That was about to change.

Two days after inheriting the Iran portfolio from Bill, I got a call from the FBI. They had just arrested a man at JFK Airport in New York who was there to meet a crew of alleged contract killers connected to Mexican drug cartels. The FBI was preparing to charge the man, an Iranian-born used-car salesman from Texas named Manssor Arbabsiar, with conspiring to murder the Saudi ambassador to the United States. It was an outlandish scheme, something out of a Hollywood movie: the Mexican hit men would be paid $15,000 to blow up the Saudi ambassador as he ate dinner at Cafe Milano, one of the trendiest restaurants in Washington, and one frequented not just by the ambassador but, on any given night, by a couple of senators, high-powered lobbyists, Washington socialites, and the occasional former president. Had Arbabsiar succeeded, it would have been a disaster, and a major international incident.

But there was more. The FBI charged another conspirator in absentia that day, Gholam Shakuri, Arbabsiar's cousin and a highly placed member of the Al-Quds Force, a division of the elite Islamic Revolutionary Guard Corps.

Fittingly, then, my first official duty as undersecretary was to reach out to our ambassadors across the globe to provide them with talking points to convince foreign capitals that the conspiracy was for real and that Iran had to be held to account.

Before I fully engaged capitals, I called in a group of intelligence analysts and Iran watchers to give me the backstory on this bizarre tale. They briefed me on everything from the history of US relations with Iran to the politics of current Iran, to the particulars of the case at hand. Before I had figured out the best route for my morning commute, I was becoming an expert in the minutiae of Iranian power factions.

◇◇◇◇◇◇◇◇◇◇◇◇

This is the leadership that President Obama attempted to reach out to, in hopes of stopping their development of a nuclear weapon. During his 2008 campaign, Obama told a debate audience that he'd be willing to talk to Iran and Syria to help quell violence in Iraq. After he was elected, Obama spoke directly to Iran, saying in his first inaugural address, "We will extend a hand if you are willing to unclench your fist."

This was a 180-degree turn from the US approach to Iran for almost a quarter-century. We'd first applied sanctions in 1984 after it was determined that the mullahs had been involved in the bombing of a US Marine barracks in Lebanon. During the Clinton administration, despite a courageous speech by Secretary of State Madeleine Albright suggesting a détente with Iran, we had banned investment in Iran's oil fields by US oil companies. President George W. Bush went after foreign entities that tried to trade with Iran.

Sanctions are often useful in bringing a misbehaving nation to the bargaining table, but they rarely if ever convince any nation to change the misbehavior itself. Most of the sanctions directed at Iran since 1984 have not only undermined its economy but deprived the country of technology that its scientists could use to make weapons. Although aimed in large part at punishing the mullahs for their pursuit of weapons, sanctions alone have done little to curb their acquisition of the elements of a bomb. When the Europeans began negotiations in earnest in 2006, Iran had 164 spinning centrifuges. When the Obama administration got deeply engaged, Iran had 19,000.

Similarly, Iran has repeatedly been threatened with force. During President George W. Bush's second term and well after (in fact, even as we sewed up the agreement with Iran), there was talk of bombing uranium-enrichment sites at Natanz and Fordow and the Arak plutonium reactor. Just as sanctions won't force any country to give up its objectionable activity, military strikes weren't going to make the Iranians forget how to make bombs; its nuclear project would be set back, but not ended. Even the advocates for bombing put the delay at three to five years.

Meanwhile, an aerial attack would give Iran justification for building an atomic device in the first place. An attack on Iran "would mean regional war," Meir Dagan, the head of Israel's intelligence service, the Mossad in those years, told *The New Yorker*. "In that case you would have given Iran the best possible reason to continue the nuclear program." And they would be likely to rebuild their facilities underground and in secret.

Despite the patent futility of war or simply continuing sanctions, no previous president had dared to literally open talks with the Iranians.

Not that President Obama was naively hoping that the Iranians would rush to dismantle the nuclear program they'd put so many resources into constructing. He took unilateral action to dissuade and delay Iran. In 2011, the *New York Times* reported that a computer virus known as Stuxnet had been released into the Iranian Atomic Energy Organization's network, crashing the country's uranium-producing centrifuges. The president commissioned, and in 2015 the Pentagon deployed, a new thirty-thousand-pound bomb that could penetrate the once-secret Fordow underground enrichment facility. His administration carried out an increasingly harsh regime of economic sanctions. But the president's goal was always to provoke a negotiation with Iran.

Before any diplomatic initiative can begin, there are questions that must be asked: Are the stated goals achievable? Are they consequential? Are there better alternatives? Will the effort, in other words, do anything worthwhile? And will the risk be worth the cost?

To these considerations, Obama was adding another dimension: can a long, bitter history be rerouted? This meant operating not solely from a position of overwhelming power but treating Iran as a party who could bargain credibly—indeed, requiring them to do so as a prerequisite of the negotiation. He was inviting the United States and Iran to drop their guard long enough to talk.

In politics, such courage is rarely applauded. It would have been easier, politically, for Obama to follow through on the threats made by the Bush White House and Israeli prime minister Benjamin Netanyahu. The American public tends to rally around any successful military mission, led by their president and their elected representatives in Congress. Our allies, too, like to see the United States using its world-leading might, if good results come.

The most effective route, however, and the hardest, is to negotiate—to use diplomacy. But it comes at a cost. Making a courageous decision, doing the right thing, always does.

chapter two

COMMON GROUND

I first formally met the men who would become my counterparts in the Iran negotiation, Abbas Araghchi and Majid Ravanchi, in September 2013 in New York, during my third UN General Assembly. It was a bonding experience unlike any other. Had we not been divided by culture, religion, and our countries' decades of enmity, we might have had a good laugh and enjoyed a thriving working relationship from the start.

Earlier that summer, the reform candidate in the Iranian elections, Hassan Rouhani, had been elected president of Iran. Rouhani had appointed as his foreign minister Javad Zarif, who had gone to college at San Francisco State University and received his doctorate in international affairs from the University of Denver. Though a dedicated supporter of the revolution—as a student, he had occupied the Iranian consulate in San Francisco to force out diplomats who were insufficiently Islamic—Zarif was comfortable with Americans and Western ways. In the early 1980s, he returned to the States to work at the Iranian mission to the United Nations and served as Tehran's ambassador to the UN for five years in the mid-2000s.

Now, as Rouhani's newly appointed foreign minister, Zarif was charging around Manhattan with a brio born of not only his new position but his usual, friendly enthusiasm when he returned to his old stomping grounds.

Araghchi and Ravanchi came along as Zarif's rather more sober deputies. Their other purpose in coming to New York was to meet with Deputy Secretary of State Bill Burns and Jake Sullivan, who had been State's director of policy planning under Hillary Clinton and now was Vice President Joe Biden's national security adviser. For some months, Burns and Sullivan, along with a small team of negotiators from State and the White House, had been secretly meeting with Araghchi and Ravanchi, the first extended talks between Iranian and American officials since the fall of the Shah.

Burns was the perfect lead for this sensitive mission. A diplomat's diplomat, and the most senior career Foreign Service officer at the time, Burns is a tall man with a basketball player's build and a trim, slightly gray mustache. He had been ambassador to Jordan and Russia and was also an arms control expert, smart beyond measure, and a highly skilled strategist and tactician who kept every move close to his chest. Jake Sullivan, who later became Hillary Clinton's chief policy adviser on her 2016 campaign, is a brilliant lawyer and indefatigable negotiator, qualities that sometimes surprised those who judged him by his looks, which put him younger even than his thirty-some years.

In 2012, Sullivan, along with a White House Middle East specialist named Puneet Talwar, had flown to the tiny Persian Gulf sultanate of Oman on the invitation of its ruler, the sultan of Oman, to meet some Iranian officials to explore the possibility of a back channel, one that would duplicate UN-sponsored multilateral sessions that had been going on since 2011. After a few follow-up encounters that convinced President Obama and Secretary of State Clinton that the Iranians were seriously responding to the president's offers to talk, Burns and Sullivan, along with a small team of technical experts, had begun meeting with the officials regularly. They began to grope their way toward extricating Iran from the jam it had gotten itself into with its nuclear program.

As our lead in the P5+1 talks and the holder of the Iran portfolio at State, I was being kept aware of Bill and Jake's progress. Now, in New York, Burns wanted to introduce me to the back channel for the first time to put names to faces in anticipation of the day when the two channels would be melded.

Using the flood of diplomats at the United Nations as a cover, the two Iranians, Burns, and Sullivan slipped away with their teams to a hotel across town, far from the proceedings at the UN. At an appointed hour, I too left my official duties at the UN, jumped into a cab without any aides in tow and joined them in Bill's suite. It was a rather stiff meeting. Araghchi and Ravanchi were very reserved, and in keeping with the customs of their conservative brand of Islam, neither could shake my hand. Nonetheless, there was an air of optimism coming from the two Iranians. They encouraged us to consider Rouhani's election a new start to the negotiations. We knew that Rouhani was already disposed to improve relations with the West. His presidential campaign's platform of "reform" was a euphemism in Iranian politics that meant relaxing the country's confrontational posture and improving the economy. Both goals were popular with voters in Iran, who blamed Mahmoud Ahmadinejad, president of Iran, for pursuing nukes while badly mismanaging the economy. Sanctions had made day-to-day life difficult for the average Iranian: many people had taken to carrying huge stacks of cash to be able to pay for ordinary household items. In January 2013, the European Union had passed a draconian batch of sanctions that in effect turned off the spigot to Iranian oil going to the West.

Rouhani had run for president on these pocketbook issues, promising to raise the standard of living. Zarif's appointment as foreign minister had served as an announcement that, unlike his predecessor, Rouhani was ready to deal. According to Ahmadinejad's foreign minister, Rouhani was astonished to learn after his election that there were one-on-one talks already going on between the United States and Iran. But Rouhani wanted to show the world that he was moving forward. Three days after his inauguration, Rouhani called for the official P5+1 talks, stalled for the Iranian election season, to start up again.

The new Iranian president also used the General Assembly to make his intentions clear. A day after meeting Araghchi and Ravanchi at Bill Burns's hotel, I had a more public encounter with the two. The P5+1, looking to capitalize on the newfound momentum, held a ministerial meeting, chaired by the high representative of the European Union, Cathy Ashton, "on the sidelines," as extracurricular talks at the GA are termed. At the U-shaped wooden table ringed with the P5+1 foreign ministers and their seconds, Zarif and John Kerry, who had by now succeeded Hillary Clinton as Obama's secretary of state, were purposely seated catty-corner from each other. It was the first time the American and Iranian foreign ministers had been in such purposeful proximity since the 1970s. The press was invited in to capture the hopeful moment for the cameras. Each of the ministers took a turn expressing their commitment to the process.

Kerry wanted something more definite, and so he had conveyed messages both through Bill Burns and via the UN ambassadors that he would be open to a **bilateral** meeting if the Iranians were. Zarif was more than ready to meet. When the official meeting ended, Kerry led Zarif into an adjacent room just big enough for the two of them to sit down and talk.

The press instantly grabbed hold of this breakthrough, just as Kerry had intended. The seemingly casual, impromptu chat was more stressful for me and my new Iranian acquaintances. For half an hour, I stood outside the door of the small meeting room with Araghchi, Ravanchi, and Hossein Fereydoun, President Rouhani's brother, as Kerry and Zarif talked inside. Both men are ebullient and chatty, and Kerry more than any diplomat on his level believes deeply in the power of personal relationships. Both men had great ambitions for a deal. Outside the door, the four of us stood nervously making small talk, wondering how far the two principals would go. We could only hope that neither would make promises beyond their writ. Though none of us shared our concern aloud, it was evident from our single look of anxious amusement that it felt like a very long half-hour.

In a stunning parallel to the Kerry-Zarif meeting, President Obama picked up the phone as the General Assembly ended and spoke briefly with President Rouhani. It became clear that the success of a deal between two nations that had not spoken for decades would henceforth rely on human connections.

These two exhilarating, historic conversations were the real beginning of the Iran talks. They set a new pace for everything that followed. Afterward, the Iranians appeared willing to speak more candidly and substantively, and when we hit a choke point, we had faith that straight talk, not white papers or habitual animosities, would get us through. On that level turf, the deal began to really run. Indeed, Kerry and Zarif often emailed each other to try out ideas in a free flow that sometimes had to be renavigated with other members of the team in order to incorporate them into the deal.

John Kerry's formal public demeanor and patrician New England vowels can make him seem a bit too elite, but he has a knack for forging common ground, and for capitalizing on it to get to a successful end. It's impossible to overstate how much Kerry's personal approach to diplomacy drove the Iran deal. Constantly taking the pulse of the individual players, Kerry put the person at the center of his negotiating strategy instead of putting protocol first, as less comfortable diplomats often do. The secretary has an instinctive understanding of social relationships, and when he is not actively negotiating at the table, he works his strong network of connections to influence, reassure, and massage those he's negotiating with, constantly seeking common ground. The secret talks themselves were a product of Kerry's personal network. In 2012, the sultan of Oman had reached out through a mutual acquaintance to Kerry when he was still chair of the Senate Foreign Relations Committee, to see if the sultan could somehow foster friendlier relations between the United States and Iran. Still, before we sent our first emissaries to talk with the Iranians, Senator Kerry went on his own to Oman, in what amounted to personal scouting trips to verify that the channel the sultan promised was actually connected on the other end to the decision-makers in Iran, including the Supreme Leader.

In the Middle East, Kerry nurtured his long friendship with Bibi Netanyahu and the trust he'd established with the Palestinian leader Mahmoud Abbas. In the Iran negotiations, he forged a strong bond with the Russian foreign minister, Sergey Lavrov, and overcame the limited English of China's Wang Yi. Before we headed to Vienna for the tortuous last month that would yield the final agreement with

Iran, Kerry and I stopped in Paris to rally all the European foreign ministers, to make sure everyone was on board for the homestretch. As he flew from one official visit to another, he never hesitated to make intermediate stops if doing so meant he could catch a few minutes with someone who could make a difference. Kerry felt that if he didn't put in the time, he would have a hard time wielding his power. You can't accomplish your goals without finding out what makes your interlocutor tick: What makes her or him laugh? What does she or he like to talk about when not talking about nuclear weapons?

There are limits to what you can accomplish by finding commonality with your adversary. Personal connections won't ever overcome substantive differences, nor should they. Before the Iranian elections ousted President Ahmadinejad, Saeed Jalili, Ahmadinejad's lead negotiator, would read out prepared statements in Farsi, followed by the translations of what Jalili had just read. Each recitation reiterated the Iranians' unshakable positions, declaring their right to develop peaceful nuclear power and the illegality of the sanctions the United Nations countries had imposed. This was the way the negotiation went through rounds in Istanbul; Baghdad; Moscow; and Almaty, Kazakhstan, as we political directors of the P5+1 and the EU sat quietly at the ubiquitous round or U-shaped table. This was apparently the way the real hardliners of Iran wanted it. They may have preferred Ahmadinejad, who relied on a conservative, populist base and made no secret of the fact that they were not anxious to deal with the Great Satan. They may have been merely stalling for time, talking in circles while every day drawing closer to being able to produce a bomb. The longer we talked, after all, the more leverage they had.

Either way, Jalili's theatrical readings of the Iranians' position were designed to keep us at arm's length and prevent common, human connection from forming lest soft spots develop in their armor against a deal. We had little choice but to endure it with diplomatic aplomb. These achingly monotonous sessions were the ultimate expression of the reality that diplomacy sometimes consists of nothing more than staying attentive, hoping to discover a way forward.

The back channel was different because it was founded on our common tie to the sultan of Oman, who was a proven conduit for both countries. Among other services he provided, the sultan had helped gain the release of American hikers who had been imprisoned in Iran in 2010. But his influence over Iran and its president had only gotten us to the table. There too it seemed as if the Iranians were negotiating only out of a sense of obligation—to the sultan this time instead of the UN. Talking to the Americans in Oman was no better than talking to them at P5+1, mandated by the UN Security Council.

Rouhani's election helped break this logjam. So did a substantive change that would put us Americans on the same footing as our allies in the P5+1. The American government's position had long been that we would not negotiate about the amount of uranium Iran could enrich. Since the first indications that Iran was enriching uranium had come to light during the Bush 43 administration, the acceptable amount of uranium the United States would allow the Iranians to have was zero. The Iranians, meanwhile, had stood on the principle that enriching uranium for civil uses, as they claimed they were doing, was their right as a sovereign nation and did not violate any treaties.

Now President Obama, seizing the opportunity offered by Rouhani's presidency, decided to jump-start the secret talks by introducing a potential way forward. He would at least entertain the possibility of very limited uranium enrichment, if it could be tightly monitored and verified. It was strongly emphasized that such a way forward was only a possibility, not a commitment. President Obama—and US policy—still held (and still does today) that no country has a right to enrich uranium. However, if the Iranians would deal, the president would consider it. He sent Bill and Jake to Oman in August with this key offer.

In practical terms, we weren't giving away much of anything. Iran had already mastered the science of making enriched uranium. They would continue to stockpile it whether we accepted their right to do so or not. If we took military action to destroy their facilities, they would rebuild the facilities, most likely underground and in secret. We couldn't bomb away their knowledge. Standing fast on the ground of no enrichment only frustrated our European partners, made them slow to impose their own sanctions, and gave Iran the opportunity to cast us as the recalcitrant party.

The new proposal, on the other hand, would give us a handle on Iran's enrichment activities, while allowing the Iranian regime to claim that they had faced down the world to retain their civil nuclear program. Their narrative of resistance would remain intact, even as they got some conditional relief from the sanctions. Strategically, they couldn't say no. Politically, they were given space to say yes.

◇◇◇◇◇◇◇◇◇◇◇◇

Before and after each round of the secret talks, Bill Burns's chief of staff would walk a sealed, unmarked manila envelope down to my chief of staff. Inside, for my eyes only, were talking points for the up-coming meeting or a summary of the last ones.

In October—a month after the General Assembly where I had met Araghchi and Ravanchi—I flew to Oman to get a read on how the talks were going. It was a curious trip. For one thing, I couldn't tell my husband where I was going or why. A car pulled up outside my home and I said good-bye. "Have a good time," he said, "wherever it is."

I flew to Dubai in the United Arab Emirates on my black diplomatic passport. At customs, I realized with rising panic that I hadn't gotten the required diplomatic visa, because my trip was supposed to be a secret. Fortunately, I had packed my personal blue passport, which did not require a special visa, and quickly switched as I presented myself as an American citizen for my flight to Oman.

When I arrived in Muscat, the low, gleaming-white capital laid out between bare desert mountains and the Gulf of Oman, I was driven to an unremarkable motel-like facility on the grounds of a guesthouse belonging to the sultan of Oman, overlooking the Gulf. Deputy Secretary of State Bill Burns, Jake Sullivan, and a handful of other diplomats and technical experts were already there, and already in the midst of a negotiating session.

In the morning, we went over to the guesthouse, a comfortable space with a conference room and outside balcony. Waiting for us was a small team of Iranian negotiators, including Araghchi and Ravanchi. The two were direct, fearsomely smart, knowledgeable, and committed to maintaining their colorless demeanor, at least while I was around. But I was getting to know them better. Ravanchi, with a relatively welcoming countenance, kept the proceedings moving along, though he proved fierce in defending his country's interests when push came to shove. Araghchi had more austere looks and an almost suspicious air, but generally deferred to Ravanchi's lead.

It was an odd feeling to be meeting so normally, yet anonymously, with representatives of a government with whom we'd been so long at odds. After exchanging greetings, we went upstairs as a group to the second floor of the villa, where we spent most of the morning of that hot day talking on a balcony with a spectacular view of the sparkling blue water. At midday, our team walked across the compound to another waterside building where a huge buffet lunch had been laid out for us. Late in the afternoon, as it cooled down, I took a short walk along the beach. I stopped to watch a few fishermen standing in the surf beside their colorfully painted boats, pulling in their nets, completely oblivious to the high-stakes negotiations going on a few hundred feet away. The picturesque scene only made my visit more surreal. The next morning we left the motel for the airport and climbed aboard an unmarked military plane to go back to Washington with the (heavily bracketed) text of an interim agreement.

◇◇◇◇◇◇◇◇◇◇

When the P5+1 negotiations resumed that November in Geneva, Switzerland, Araghchi and Ravanchi had replaced Jalili as the top negotiators for Iran, now led by Foreign Minister Javad Zarif. But there was a difference from how they operated in the back channel. Araghchi was now the chief negotiator, with Ravanchi as his second. Ravanchi's portfolio in the Iranian foreign service included the United States, and since we were the only country at the back-channel talks, he had taken the lead in Oman. Araghchi, who was responsible for international matters, had now naturally stepped forward in the United Nations talks. But we assumed that Araghchi had another qualification to be Iran's public face in the UN talks: unlike Ravanchi or even Zarif, Araghchi was a veteran of the 1979 revolution. Ironically, we also realized that Araghchi had been on Jalili's delegation, but we had not gotten to know him. In a sign of how distant those talks had been, we hadn't even realized that he spoke perfect English.

As we started the P5+1 negotiations anew, I felt that it was crucial to carry over the same sense of connection in our day-to-day inter-action with the Iranians that Kerry had established with Zarif. I had a significant problem, however, in that I still could not shake hands with my counterparts.

Conservative Muslims in many cultures are forbidden by cus-tom from physical contact with members of the opposite sex, how-ever incidental. In Iran, the sexes are segregated in public, sitting in separate rows on buses and trains and in university classrooms. These rules don't evaporate when Iranians cross the border, not even when they enter worlds where a handshake can mean a great deal. Diplo-mats and other frequent travelers to the Middle East have developed a work-around: those of us who are barred from shaking hands press our right hands to our chests and give a slight nod. It does the job, though when you're the only woman in a roomful of men, repeatedly clasping your chest and nodding, you often risk looking like you're stuck in a Marx Brothers routine.

In a negotiation as consequential, difficult, and long as this one promised to be, you need to lower the barriers between you and your adversary. Establishing a common sense of mission and shared suc-cess is crucial. Unexpectedly, this make-do gesture provided me with a great opening to address the cultural differences between me and the Iranians.

One day early in the reestablished talks, during a break in a nego-tiating session, I turned the conversation with Araghchi and Ravan-chi toward our inability to shake hands. I explained that I had grown up in a Jewish neighborhood outside Baltimore, and that many of my neighbors were strictly observant Orthodox Jewish families. Just as in conservative Islam, the Orthodox are not permitted to touch anyone of the opposite sex besides their spouse, child, or parent.

Araghchi and Ravanchi were at first slightly mortified to have their behavior become a point of discussion, but as I told my story they were fascinated. They'd never known that they shared this custom with Judaism—understandably perhaps, since fewer than ten thousand Jews are thought to still live in Iran. One of them, they told me, was a representative in parliament, a fact that I found more than ironic given Iranian denials of the Holocaust. Talking about the awkwardness of our greeting transformed its significance. These two Iranians knew more about my background. They could see me a little better, not just as a representative of the United States, or as an untouchable member of the opposite sex, but as a human being with a history and an appreciation for their cultural norms. After this, we still bowed instead of shaking hands, but the fact that we could not shake hands became not an obstacle but a point of commonality.

Establishing common ground with the Iranians was especially important precisely because our cultures were so different. In many negotiations, much can be achieved in casual meetings away from the official sessions—when those at loggerheads go out for a smoke during a break, or happen to take the same elevator or split a taxi, or above all when they sit down for dinner together. The Islamic ban on alcohol consumption prevented us from inviting the Iranians to dine with us, since wine was served in our dining room—a requirement of the European contingent. In the early going, the Iranians were wary about extending a dinner invitation to us. This was a real check on building rapport away from the negotiating table and fostering relaxed conversation. But as the deal, and the two sides, got closer, Zarif, very social and expansive by nature, began to invite us to talk over meals. That was an indication to us that we were getting closer to a deal. We were always happy to accept, not least because their dishes— my mouth still waters at the memory of the Persian chicken with pistachios—were uniformly fantastic.

Equally complicated, if not more so, was the political divide— really a psychological divide—between the Western teams and the Iranians. For several reasons, it was not uncommon for the Iranians to suddenly pull back from an agreed-upon position or to become visibly tortured about some point we were discussing. For one thing, the professional and even personal stakes were much higher for their negotiating team than for ours. If the US team failed to come up with a deal with the Iranians, or if our political opposition called us appeasers or the deal treasonous (and they did and continue to do so), our careers would not be over and our reputations would probably survive. Our country would face a greater threat, but average Americans wouldn't feel it immediately in their pocketbooks. The Iranians could count on no such assurances.

Another factor was what has been called Iran's culture of resistance. The Iranians bridled constantly at being told by the former colonial powers what kind of weapons they could have. The British and Americans had a history, from the Iranian perspective, of treating Middle East countries as our fiefs or domains. We had organized a coup against their leaders. We had created client states and spread chaos, in the Iranians' view, for the sake of cheap oil prices and high dividends. For them, nearly everyone at the opposing table represented the first-world corruption that their revolution stood against. Bowing to the wishes of these world powers betrayed their sense of who they were. Their pose of resistance led them at times to irrational positions. When we offered them relief from sanctions, they claimed that the sanctions weren't hurting them. It was a preposterous pose, but one that was vital to their self-regard.

This narrative of resistance haunted the entire negotiation, at times driving us to shouting matches or ultimatums. Some of their emotional moments—Zarif wasn't above abruptly leaving the table at difficult spots, saying he had to pray, or clutching his temples—were calculated and purely tactical, as were ours. When your approach to a negotiation is that your very survival as a nation is at stake, it explains a lot of behaviors.

Calling them out for their skillful use of shenanigans produced a tough moment for me early in the negotiations. At a Senate Foreign Relations Committee hearing in 2013, responding to a question from a senator about whether we could trust the Iranians to keep up their side of a bargain, I replied that "deception is in their DNA." The Iranians took that comment as a slur on their negotiation team. Iranian newspapers ran cartoons of me as a fox perched in a tree. (This image later, along with my silver hair, became the basis for Team Silver Fox, emblazoned by one of my team on T-shirts for us all.) Iranians took to the street shouting "Death to Wendy Sherman," unnerving my family. When I did an interview with Voice of America Persian, I set up a question beforehand with my interviewer about the exchange so that I'd have an opportunity to express my regret for any offense my DNA comment had caused. However, later in the negotiation, when Iran used words that offended me, I was able to use this painful moment to make a point back to them. When they were playing the victim card, protesting that some point or another was an example of prejudicial distrust, I had a victim card of my own to lay down. Ironically, my infamy in the streets of Iran gave us a common language of being persecuted.

Whether we bought the Iranians' political culture or not, we needed to understand the dynamics of it, and we needed a glue that would bind them to the process and keep them coming back to the table. We had to understand where they were coming from.

Opportunities to deescalate tension are always in short supply at the negotiating table. As a negotiator, you're looking for something to discuss that won't lead to mutual criticism or take you away from the matter at hand.

We did succeed in developing connections with the Iranians. Some were based on happy coincidences. At a crucial juncture in the negotiation, the Iranians brought in Ali Salehi, the head of their Atomic Energy Organization, to anchor their technical team and scrutinize the tiniest details of what was being proposed. We answered with Secretary of Energy Ernest Moniz. It turned out that Moniz had taught at the Massachusetts Institute of Technology in Cambridge when Salehi was getting a graduate degree there, and though they hadn't known each other, having MIT in common was the basis of a wonderful rapport. When news came during the talks that Salehi had become a grandfather, Moniz showed up at the next round with a baby onesie with "MIT" emblazoned across the chest. Ernie's and Salehi's mutual regard became an invaluable strength for the P5+1 team in those final weeks.

In the end, we just spent too much time together not to begin to see each other's human side. We related to each other's aches and pains—Foreign Minister Zarif's constantly bothersome back, a broken nose I suffered when I ran into a glass door running to answer a phone call, Secretary Kerry's broken femur from a bicycle accident. Breaks in formal sessions were often passed in explaining the intricacies of our ailments. We treated each other with mercy. When Salehi had surgery, he gamely phoned in to a meeting in Geneva, but he sounded so weak and was in such evident discomfort that we agreed as a group that he should hang up.

We even had occasion to grieve with the Iranians. Just a few months before the end of negotiations, the mother of President Rouhani and Hossein Fereydoun passed away. We took a break from negotiating so that everyone on the Iranian side could go home for the funeral. Before they left, the American delegation paid a visit to Fereydoun, who was with us in Lausanne. Our condolences were as heartfelt as if we'd been offering them to one of our own colleagues. A mother is a mother, no matter where you're from.

As a result, the Iran negotiations became as personally integrated a diplomatic effort as I've worked on, especially considering the divisions we began with. Forging common bonds doesn't mean ceding ground unnecessarily or out of empathy. On the contrary, the familiarity we developed was patently useful. Over time I learned to tell which of Zarif's dramatic turns were for effect and which meant he was truly upset, and thus whether I should strike a conciliatory tone by addressing him as "Javad" or call him "Minister," by which he would know that I was ticked off and not buying his dramatics.

The picture we have of negotiations is often that of a set-to between antagonists. In fact, the most successful negotiations I've been a part of have operated with a responsibility to the group. Fostering cohesion by building relationships creates norms, and norms change minds. You create a norm of wanting to get to success. "We will never get to peace" becomes "We must get to peace." This is how groups work. No matter how disparate its members, a group that builds common ground develops its own center of gravity. It then begins to move in a single direction.

Establishing human ties can only lead to better negotiations. So much of coming to an agreement is learning the true nature of the opposite side's concerns, and to do this we need to see what drives them. It's likely to be a need that we share and that can be used to deepen our mutual respect and develop a sense of common cause. Deep into the Iran negotiations, amid the toughest days in fact, Araghchi and I happened to be sorting out some contentious point just as my daughter sent me a couple of snapshots of her infant son on my phone. Soon we found ourselves sharing pictures of our grand-children, both having just become grandparents for the first time. For a few minutes, we were having a normal conversation, asking one another: How many? How old? What's this one's name?

We had struck upon a completely permissible subject for nonthreatening conversation. Amid the host of topics, nuclear and non-nuclear, cultural and political, that we could not talk about, Araghchi and I made a permanent human connection. Years after the end of the negotiations, Araghchi still sends me a greeting at Christmastime, and I send him greetings at Nowruz, the Iranian New Year. Although I don't, as a Jew, celebrate Christmas, I do appreciate the holiday sentiment. We don't know how our human connections may yet serve the world.

◇◇◇◇◇◇◇◇◇◇

My experience with Iran was not the first time I'd had to navigate an alien culture. In the early 1970s, I spent two years as a young men-tal health worker in Savannah, Georgia. Savannah is not so far from Maryland—a long day's drive down Interstate 95. Until I got to the Deep South, I hadn't thought of myself as a Yankee exactly; it's not uncommon to hear a "y'all" even in downtown Baltimore. But my

time in Savannah was my first foray outside my comfortable, even
sheltered, world—Baltimore's primarily Jewish suburb of Pikesville—
which the comfort of the cloistered world of college had done little
to disturb. Stepping outside my world taught me some hard lessons
about differences—albeit differences not as dramatic as those with
Iran, but instructive for that challenge later in life.

I was a year out of college, already married to my high school boyfriend, Alfred, who had recently finished law school and secured a job
with Georgia Legal Services. As soon as he graduated, in June 1972,
we packed up our small apartment in Boston and drove south in our
boxy, mustard-colored Volvo. We pulled up to our new place in one
of Savannah's picturesque city squares, the trees hung with Spanish
moss, feeling very far from home.

That year was a tense time for the country, and not an ideal
moment for a pair of outsiders to find their feet in a new world.
Though the Watergate break-in had just begun to make the papers,
for the moment President Nixon was running for reelection. Vietnam
was an increasingly desperate war zone, however, and he was faced
with antiwar demonstrations outside the Republican National Convention hall in Miami. The Republicans' "Southern Strategy," as it
later came to be known, purposely pitted angry white voters below
the Mason-Dixon Line against the Democratic left, whose candidate,
Senator George McGovern, had already been nominated in another
roiling convention in Chicago. That spring Alabama governor George
Wallace, campaigning for president in Laurel, Maryland, near my
family home in Columbia, had been shot and paralyzed below the
waist in an assassination attempt.

Amid all this turmoil, the town of Savannah was an island of ante-
bellum grace. Savannahians seemed to have an instinct for insulating

themselves with a profound sense of belonging. For outsiders like Alfred and me, this insularity could be disconcerting. Soon after we got to town, I read in the local paper about a woman who had recently died at the age of ninety-three, having moved to Savannah at the age of three. Her obituary began, "Although not a native Savannahian...." As a "Northerner," and a progressive, antiwar feminist at that, I wondered how I would be seen in this place where ninety years of residency still qualified you as a newcomer.

It would not take me long to find out. I took a job in my chosen field of community mental health. This was the era of deinstitutionalization, when chronically mentally ill patients across the country who had been kept in large mental hospitals were being reintegrated into their communities. Georgia's governor, Jimmy Carter, had created community mental health centers across the state to help support them. I was hired at Savannah's center to run a twenty-four-hour crisis hotline established for the troubled or suicidal.

Most days I trained and managed the volunteers who answered the phones, but once a month or so I drove out with my outreach partner, John, to visit a public health office in Springfield, Georgia, and make home visits in nearby Egypt. We would check in on patients' medications or make sure high school kids who were having problems were connected to the resources they needed. Then we would drive back, a circuit of about fifty miles through rural Georgia.

These trips deepened my feeling of having fallen into a different dimension. Every car we passed on the two-lane highways seemed to be a pickup truck, and it seemed as if every truck had a shotgun in the rack in its back-cabin window. My Volvo, meanwhile, was something of a spectacle. When we'd stop at a gas station, people would come running out to see the "furrin" car.

My partner and I were a curiosity as well. John was African American, also in his twenties, and the sight of him riding in a car with a young white woman made many Georgians of the time uneasy. If race relations in this part of Georgia in the early '70s were not particularly tense, it was only because no one challenged the social order that had stood unchanged since the days of Jim Crow. At the public health office in Springfield, a sliding accordion wall divided the waiting room in two. There was no sign explicitly designating one side or the other "whites only," but somehow the African American patients knew to come in the back door and sit in their part of the waiting room. The white patients entered through the front door and sat in their waiting area. John and I disrupted the local custom by eating together at Ethel's, the main diner in Springfield. I didn't think to do any differently.

I don't know what John's experience was like, whether at Ethel's or riding with me around rural Georgia. We never talked about it, or for that matter about our personal lives or our feelings about doing our jobs. It's a sad commentary on the time and on ourselves. It never occurred to me to find out more about where this other person was coming from culturally. If it was at times difficult for him, or if he'd felt threatened, he never mentioned it, but now, years later, I see that just mentioning any discomfort he felt might have been threatening to his job. Later I found out that the public health nurses had been trying to get the two of us kicked out of the public health office for the entire first year that we came to Springfield.

My alienation was not restricted to matters of race. One day a young woman came into the community mental health center in Savannah asking to talk with someone. I took her back to one of the offices where we did intake interviews and asked what kind of help she was looking for. For nearly an hour she talked to me about how her husband abused her. Recently, she told me, he had tried to smother her with a pillow. I was shocked and indignant. I don't recall if we used the word "battered" in those days, but I can tell you it was the first time I'd knowingly sat with a battered woman.

My inexperience showed. Rather than really hear her, I immediately began trying to fix her situation. I explained the resources available for her so that she could leave her husband.

She never came back to see me again, and that experience has haunted me ever since. I realized, too late, that she wasn't ready to leave her husband. In such a small, conservative, and deeply religious community, she would have faced enormous social pressure to forgive him and reunite with him. She also would probably have had to forgo whatever financial comfort she had. The woman had really only wanted to know if there was anything that would make staying with her husband better. She had been looking for someone to listen and help her think, not take command of her next steps.

I had projected onto her what I thought I'd want if I were in her shoes. It's the opposite of the precept I later learned in social work school, both as a community organizer and as a clinician. Start with where the client is. Recognizing the cultural or psychological pressures on the person in front of you is an essential beginning to any relationship.

It was in Savannah too that I learned the power of group dynamics. Consciousness-raising may sound quaint to anyone who didn't live through the liberation movements of the 1960s and '70s—a combination of hippie New Age expression and tentative self-discovery. Nonetheless, it was what we did back then. Not long after I had arrived, one of my coworkers at the mental health center and I founded a women's consciousness-raising group. It was intended as nothing more than a sane place for a dozen or so of us "ex-pats," as we called ourselves, to find some solace and get advice about how to cope in this culture we so little understood. We had no planned activities or assigned readings. We met informally in each other's houses about once a week and talked. We were all far from our parents, doing things they had never shown us how to do. The group helped us trade ideas, expand our networks, and give each other mutual support. Word of mouth drew in some local women too, which made the group more whole, and more interesting.

For Savannah at the time, any group of women meeting without input from their husbands was pretty radical. Few of the local women were looking for empowerment per se. Some were desperate simply to find a safe place to talk—these weren't women for whom it was permissible to go see a therapist or psychiatrist. One local woman, no matter which birth control method she used, repeatedly ended up pregnant— even when she was on the Pill, with its 98 percent success rate.

But all of us, ex-pats and natives, were crashing through traditional cultural bounds. One woman who was very unhappy in her marriage ended up having an affair with another woman in the group. I won't say it was shocking in those days of the sexual revolution, but in a time before LGBTQ was appended to any list of social identities, their relationship showed how people felt safe to take bold steps in our little group.

Everyone helped move the group forward and got something in turn from it. I interacted for the first time with women my age who were already mothers. I came to understand their lives. They saw what life was like for a young professional like me who was less concerned with making a home than making change. What we saw each other going through made that life more possible for ourselves. Our differences were what made the group so powerful.

The P5+1 team, though significantly more sophisticated and mature than my cohort back in Savannah, was effective for the same reasons that group was. We brought different experiences and agendas to the table, while being conscious that we all needed each other. All six nations on the team and the EU representatives were adamant that Iran not get the bomb. But beneath that unifying principle lay disparate motivations. Each member had something different they had to get out of the talks. The Europeans, along with their primary interest of security, wanted to reopen the oil trade and resume what had been for them very lucrative commercial activity with Iran. The United States, as the world's superpower and cop-by-default, felt ultimately responsible for making sure that Iran's new freedoms didn't give it a free hand to threaten our allies in the Middle East, a threat that would be even greater with a nuclear weapon. Russia and China, both of which had maintained stronger ties with Iran, wanted the relationship to survive the deal-making process. They also believed, as a matter of principle and self-protection, that none of us should interfere in the affairs of a sovereign nation.

Additionally, I was struck by how disparate the teams all were personally. The teams of the six nations and the European Union employed diplomats and nuclear scientists, government lifers and appointees from academia and law, introverted thinkers and gregarious deal-makers. These people represented an incredible range of viewpoints, and we had crisscrossing histories and alliances. There was sometimes an understandable split between the nuclear experts— particularly in the French delegation, which was dominated by professional nonproliferation experts—and the more diplomatically minded political directors. There was a constant, and fruitful, push and pull between the unbending purists and the politicians who demanded real-world accommodations.

For all our differences, we understood that getting to an agreement could not be achieved without the other side, and that the durability of any agreement would be guaranteed only if each member's interests and needs were met, while never compromising the fundamental objective that Iran never obtain a nuclear weapon.

We were fortunate, in a sense, that the Iranians took so long before Rouhani's election in the summer of 2013 to negotiate in good faith, and especially that they took such obvious pleasure in yanking us all over the globe. After each round of negotiations, Cathy Ashton's deputy, Helga Schmid, would spend weeks negotiating the site of the next meeting with Jalili's number two, Ali Bagheri. It was a torturous game of forcing us to come to what they perceived as their territory and making the continuation of the negotiation as uncomfortable as possible for us.

It all worked to our advantage in the long run, providing a good example of how nothing in a negotiation is really wasted time. Adverse circumstances inevitably bring people together. As we flew from place to place, working together early and late, treading water for months, waiting for a break in the negotiations, we learned which teams worked best in the morning and which got their best brainstorming done over wine or a beer after a long day of formal negotiation. We found out who needed breaks to have a smoke and who needed to constantly check back with their minister for instructions. Our mutual discoveries inevitably brought us together, not just as representatives of nations with common goals but as people.

Our time together gave me the gift of at least one bona fide friendship. Helga Schmid was just one of the extraordinary women who led talks, an uncommon reversal that was a gift in itself. A quite tall, beautiful, blond woman who wore colorful long scarfs, Helga earned my admiration with her supreme organizational skills, mastery of technical detail, and capacity for hard work, all of which I pride myself on. As the talks went on, we leaned on each other, often seeking the respite of honest conversation in the ladies' room or over a glass of wine late at night in one of our rooms. During the stress of our final run at the Coburg, we found solace in retail therapy—at a Viennese dress shop just outside the back door of the hotel whose elegant merino wool dress jackets seemed designed to meet the needs of a female diplomat: they packed easily and kept one warm. In the space of twenty minutes, we did serious damage to our bank accounts.

As the Iranians stonewalled in the early rounds, we found that frustration can be a powerful force to bring people together. Anxiety works nicely as well. The most memorable of the early P5+1 rounds was the one held in 2012 in Baghdad, at a time when the Iraqi capital was still a simmering war zone. The Iranians, who were already tightening their grip on the country through their sponsorship of its powerful Shi'ite militias, were very comfortable in Iraq. The rest of us were less so, it's fair to say, for logistical reasons as much as safety concerns: commercial flights into Iraq were few and far between and subject to change. Rather than risk showing up late to the meeting (or coming early and spending a night amid the uneasy security of Baghdad), the negotiators coming to meet the Iranians flew into Amman, Jordan, and made the short flight to Bagram Air Base on US military airplanes. As we were wrapping up the round, held at a guesthouse belonging to the Iraqi prime minister's office, we noticed a whooshing sound coming from outside. Soon, the tall windows had become blanketed with an oatmeal-colored sand, obscuring the view. A few minutes later, an Iraqi official came into the meeting room to announce that a sandstorm had kicked up. All flights out of the airport would be delayed. In a perfect bookend to our unorthodox flight into the country, we spent the next few hours sitting by our luggage in the atrium of the hotel, waiting to get out.

I still keep a framed picture of the unusual sight of senior officials from China, Russia, the European Union, and the United States taking their seats on the same small plane to Baghdad, all in the care of US military pilots. The group has the jolly if uncertain look of a bunch of campers getting on the bus, ready for a summer of awkward but character-building togetherness.

<><><><><><><><>

The relationship that proved most tendentious—and quite crucial to the completion of the deal—was that between the United States and Russia. Since the Soviet Union collapsed in the 1980s, the two countries have cooperated in some areas that were once Cold War battlefields. In space, for instance, American astronauts have shared the International Space Station with Russian cosmonauts, getting there on Russian rockets. Back on Earth, however, Russia and the United States are increasingly at odds, pushing against each other's traditional spheres of influence in eastern Europe and the Middle East. Our conflicts in cyberspace have become particularly concerning. Friction over Russia's invasion of Ukraine and its support of Syrian president Bashar Al-Assad have brought our relations to a post–Cold War low.

The fate of the Iran talks could have been quite different had not the Russian team been headed up by two professional and experienced, albeit wily, diplomats. The Russian foreign minister, Sergey Lavrov, is a formidable presence: direct to the point of impatience, often charming, with a quick wit that seems at odds with his sculpted undertaker's face. His deputy, Sergey Ryabkov, is very much Lavrov's opposite, with blond hair, a broad face framed in modish eyeglasses, and a modern, European mien. Ryabkov is a specialist in western Europe and the United States, and thanks to the years he spent at the Russian embassy in Washington in the early 2000s, his English is impeccable. (Whenever we were unsure about a word that was going into a document, we'd half-jokingly turn to Ryabkov for a ruling—usually causing the British to intervene with what they considered the proper phrasing.)

I first came to appreciate Ryabkov's skill at a G8 meeting, the annual conference of the heads of state of the world's largest economies (now the G7, after Russia was disinvited following its incursions into Crimea and Ukraine), held in Northern Ireland in 2013. It was an atypically tense gathering of the G8, overshadowed by the still bubbling and nearby conflict between the Irish Republican Army (IRA) and their enemy Unionists, both of which groups had threaten to disrupt the meetings with protests or even violence. The diplomacy was troubled too by the war in Syria, which was then reaching new heights of chaos every week.

I was the top US diplomat accompanying President Obama at the meeting. At the end of the two days of the summit, I met with the seven other political directors to write the official communiqué summarizing what had been agreed on foreign policy. The problem was that when it came to Syria, nobody had really agreed on anything. The United States and most of our European allies wanted to press for Assad to resign, and we wanted to take a firm stand on inspections of his chemical weapons stores, which he had already shown he wasn't above using. The Russians fought both of these points ardently.

Ryabkov and I now had the most to say about what would go in the communiqué about the conflict. With the skilled British political director Simon Gass sitting between us, we went toe-to-toe debating the future of Assad. Ryabkov's tenacity and smarts raised the level of my game as well, and the hard-fought session went until two in the morning. I had to stand up for my own talent as a negotiator and for my country, as well as defend our points as valiantly as I could. In a warped kind of way, it was almost fun.

A few months later, Assad did use chemical weapons on his own people again, and in the ensuing crisis Ryabkov and I were thrown together again, seconding Secretary of State John Kerry and his Russian counterpart, Foreign Minister Sergey Lavrov, in a long weekend of emergency meetings in Geneva. Each of the ministers brought large teams of technical experts, but the ministers, along with Ryabkov and me, buttressed by our lawyers and representatives to the Organization for the Prohibition of Chemical Weapons (OPCW), formed the core.

Again, meals mattered. Kerry, Lavrov, Ryabkov, and I shared an early dinner to discuss core principles, aided by scotch and wine. Our teams of experts, each with their own intelligence, ultimately agreed on the amount of declared materials, a crucial parameter for resolution of the crisis. Other technical details—how to transport the chemicals, where they would go, how they would be disposed of, how the process would be verified—were all considered and resolved. The final sticking point was how the UN Security Council would act if Syria was found not in compliance with the agreement. We insisted that the resolution be under Chapter VII of the UN resolution, which allows for all necessary means. After much debate, Kerry and Lavrov migrated out of the formal meeting rooms to a small square table on the deck of the hotel swimming pool. Ryabkov and I quickly joined them, and the four of us, led by the ministers, finally agreed that the compliance section of the agreement, if not the whole agreement, would come under Chapter VII.

The result was UN Resolution 2118, passed unanimously by the UN Security Council a few short days later, requiring Assad to give up his declared chemical weapons. Though partly undone later by Assad's treachery in producing more sarin gas and attacking his people again, the resolution was a huge win at the time and one that gave Lavrov and Kerry, as well as Ryabkov and me, irreplaceable mutual respect.

By the time we met at the P5+1 negotiations, Ryabkov and I had formed, if not a friendship exactly, then a respect for the way we played the game. I soon found, however, that he had lessons to teach me about just how important it was to keep that mutual regard intact.

In August 2014, as we were meeting at the Palais Coburg in Vienna, Russian president Vladimir Putin sent troops and tanks into eastern Ukraine. Russia's aggressive move shocked the world. Throughout the last days of 2013 and into the new year, Russians had been filtering into Ukraine, disguising their troops in unmarked uniforms and tanks with hidden insignia. The Kremlin denied the existence of these "little green men," as the unidentified Russian forces were cheekily called by locals, and the whole escapade seemed like a farce. Putin was testing how far he could push the West. Now he had brazenly moved into a sovereign country. The world order seemed to have been rearranged overnight.

The next day we gathered in the ornate room where we'd been meeting at the Coburg. As we milled about the three-sided open square table and colleagues secured their espressos and nibbled at pastries, I was fuming. The Russians' action in Ukraine was so egregious, so outrageous, that I decided I had to say something to Ryabkov.

You can have very private conversations in a crowded room. A secret meeting in plain sight, in fact, can be a more effective way to get a point across than an official meeting, which requires couching your feelings in diplomatic language. At the Coburg, I went over to Ryabkov and confronted him quietly. "Sergey, what are you doing?" He looked at me for a second until he was sure he knew what I was talking about. Then he simply said, "There is nothing amiss," and walked away.

It was a lesson for which I'm still grateful to the Russian deputy minister. If Ryabkov had stayed, he'd have said all the things I didn't want to hear, and we would have had a fight, which wasn't in the interest of preventing Iran from having a nuclear weapon. Sometimes you can't have everything on the table all at once and achieve your core objective. Sometimes compartmentalizing is key. Talking about the deal at hand can require not talking about everything else.

What Ryabkov's answer told me in that moment, however, was that the Russian contingent was as committed to the group's goals as anyone, putting them above the power struggles outside the negotiating room. The right and wrong of Ukraine would have to be settled at another time. Just then we had a job to do.

chapter three

POWER

In October 2013, soon after my quiet trip to Oman, I boarded a plane to Brussels for what was supposed to be a routine prep session for the next negotiating round with the Iranians, scheduled for two weeks later in Geneva. I followed my usual ritual designed to induce sleep in an airline seat on my frequent overnight flights—express dinner with a glass of red wine, then a blanket over my head while I meditated on the image of myself in my kayak on a lake in the Berkshires. But I couldn't dispel a slight feeling of dread. I knew this meeting in Brussels would be anything but routine. I had news for my P5+1 colleagues that would completely shake up this meeting and, I had no doubt, the gathering in Geneva too.

More than a year after green-lighting secret negotiations with the Iranians, President Obama had decided it was time to reveal the back channel to the world. It fell to me to explain to my P5+1 colleagues that the Iranians and the United States were well down the road to an interim nuclear deal. Secretary Kerry and the president would be calling foreign ministers and government leaders, but the White House thought the announcement should begin quietly with the political directors who were involved in the day-to-day negotiations.

Telling my fellow political directors about the back channel was a relief for me personally. Whenever I met with the White House, or with Secretary of State Kerry or Deputy Secretary Bill Burns, I had been voicing my concern that it was past time to tell our partners about the clandestine negotiations. It was an argument I always lost. Not until Bill and Jake Sullivan had negotiated the complete shape of a provisional agreement, with only the most contentious clauses "bracketed"—drafted but not finalized—did the White House agree that it was time to share their efforts.

This was the news I was on my way to Brussels to divulge. It wasn't just the fact that we'd kept what we considered the "real" negotiations with the Iranians a secret. What made what I had to say even more delicate was what Burns and Sullivan's proposed agreement contained.

Among those bracketed portions was a provision that would allow Iran to pursue very limited enrichment of uranium—the development of quantities consistent with peaceful uses, like medical testing and civil nuclear energy. In return, Iran would submit to intensely rigorous inspections of their enrichment facilities by the neutral experts of the International Atomic Energy Agency (IAEA).

This proposal would stun the P5+1 nations. Not that they would disagree with it. On the contrary, the European Union nations, as well as Russia and China, had long seen the wisdom of permitting Iran a token amount of enrichment—enough to allow them to say that the nuclear program they'd been boasting about domestically was nominally intact. A limited enrichment program would grant the Iranian negotiators room to give ground on more important points.

The United States, however, going back to George W. Bush's administration, had always remained adamantly opposed.

Now I was going to explain to my colleagues that this was precisely what the president had agreed to, even as I had held out for—and Iran had droned on about—the no-enrichment stance of the United States at official session after official session.

I wasn't concerned about admitting that they were right, or that I'd betrayed what we'd agreed to at the public talks. (Nothing much *had* been agreed to.) Most everything in the secret provisional agreement, not just the question of limited enrichment, was aligned with their public positions. By advancing the ball in secret, we were saving them untold time and anguish.

What worried me as my plane taxied and took off was the common ground I'd forged with everyone in the P5+1 delegations, with my European partners especially. Over the past two years and more, our relationships had been based on many honest conversations about what each of us required to get to a final agreement. I was going to have to explain why we'd been holding out on them for the better part of a year.

The politics of the moment were trickier than they looked. My news would not only surprise our partners but force them to confront what they suspected already: positioned in between the United States and Iran, they had unequal status. This was an impression we tried to counter once the secret talks had been revealed. We never made a major move that didn't involve the P5+1, and almost without fail, we included Ashton, Mogherini, or, more often, Helga Schmid in any bilateral we held.

But there was more than a little truth to the idea that the nuclear talks were fundamentally between the United States and Iran. And for good reason. The world would expect the United States, still the reigning superpower, to enforce any nuclear agreement reached with Iran with a realistic threat of sanctions. Alternatively, if a deal escaped us, it would be up to the United States to take military action to stop Iran from gaining a bomb—to put our blood and treasure on the line. The deal was ours to make, even if we couldn't make it alone.

And it was in many respects our deal to make. It was "Death to America" that was chanted at Friday prayers in Tehran, not "Death to the United Nations" or any other country. It was our history and theirs that were entwined in bitter resentments. Our president had already spent a good deal of political capital to move beyond that history and that narrative.

The Iranians themselves recognized that the real negotiation was with the United States. "If we hadn't negotiated with the US, the reality was, we wouldn't have reached a deal with the P5+1," Ali Salehi, the head of Iran's Atomic Energy Organization, told the press months later. "Who else was willing to spend this amount of time and energy to negotiate with their secretaries of state and energy and experts with us?"

"We couldn't have moved forward with the others," Salehi added.

Part of what Salehi acknowledged was the simple fact that no other nation has the capacity we have. No one can rival the depth and breadth of our diplomatic team at State, with embassies ready to marshal our arguments in capitals around the globe; the financial reach of the Office of Foreign Assets Control at Treasury; the deliberative and analytic capability of the National Security Council staff at the White House; and the diligent work of the intelligence community to monitor activity inside other countries and help to certify compliance. No other country has a military that provides such a credible threat of force in service to diplomacy. Most importantly, we have the institutional infrastructure to write an entire long-term nuclear agreement in exquisite detail and enforce it over years. Despite this bureaucratic muscle, we also have the agility to pull off a chemical weapons deal like the one we did in Syria in a matter of days. Everyone hates that the United States is the sole superpower, but they don't deny it either. It's what gives us the credibility to lead in the world. (And it is why the current hollowing out of the State Department in the name of efficiency demonstrates a misunderstanding of the department's real value.)

These were all reasons for the United States to take the lead position in any negotiation with Iran. What all these reasons pointed to, however—what was really at stake in my upcoming conversation with my P5+1 colleagues—was a recognition of US power. We were the biggest player on this stage. And I had the burden of representing the sheer might of the United States.

How is it that power can be a burden? It's true that, in any negotiation, power is the primary resource. One side will almost always outweigh the other in economic strength, political pull, or military or physical muscle. Often, as in the case of the P5+1 partners, some members who are on the same side will possess more power than others.

But power is a complicated tool, and negotiations rarely come down to a simple calculation of who has more of it. History repeatedly shows that weaker countries can leverage moral claims, make short-term threats, leverage the impatience of the greater power, or, of course, resort to terror to get favorable terms. Even the most dominant states must know how to work the levers of their power, to reach out to allies to solidify their advantage, and sometimes to cede some power, tactically, to the weaker side.

In short, the Iran nuclear agreement could never have been concluded without our P5+1 partners. On the contrary, the genius of the deal was that it gave Iran nowhere in the world to turn to evade its provisions. By the same token, it made it harder for any one nation to unravel the agreement, though US power confers weight in that regard, given our economic and military might.

This was an essential feature of the deal. The United States wielded its own power by holding out the ultimate threat of military action, as is often the case in diplomacy. More immediately, and practically, we were marshaling the combined economic power of the P5+1 and the EU nations to apply pressure on Iran through sanctions. We even wanted Iran to retain some power. We were concerned that President Rouhani be left with enough authority within his government to carry out the terms of the bargain. The trick, as always, was to use power without depriving everyone else of theirs.

<><><><><><><>

A quick detour here to discuss secrecy in negotiations over time. How information is shared and power is used has changed a lot in diplomacy over the past century. Once upon a time when communications were less immediate and secrecy was more possible, private, if not clandestine, negotiations were much more common. After the First World War, there was a call for an end to secret negotiations, and secret diplomacy was often cited as a cause of the war, the kings, emperors, and empresses of Europe having locked themselves into secret agreements about mutual defense. After the war, President Woodrow Wilson announced that the days of secret negotiations were over. As time went on, secrecy came to be associated with states that were in a weak position; they kept their negotiations secret because they were playing one enemy off another.

Obviously, the United States didn't prefer secrecy with Iran out of weakness or because we depend on surprise. We never would have concluded a comprehensive deal without the other P5+1 nations or without the review by Congress. Rather, our need for secrecy was principally based on our lack of trust in Iran. If our preliminary one-on-one talks had broken down, we didn't want the failure to spread to the multilateral effort already going on. By keeping it secret, we could insulate the UN-backed talks from the animosities and mistrust that made communication between our two nations so difficult.

In this way, the back channel operated as a kind of steam valve that allowed us to discuss critical questions with Iran more directly than in the hubbub of the main talks. In Geneva, we had to sneak Bill and Jake through the hotel's kitchen to reach a meeting with Zarif to keep their presence a secret. When I sat in, I had to employ similar tactics. One night in Geneva I left the Intercontinental Hotel, the negotiation venue, to walk to a gas station, where I was picked up in a black car and whisked off to the bilateral with Bill, Jake, and the Iranians.

Negotiating privately also gave both us and the Iranians the freedom to take more risks. We could try out new ideas while insulating them from partisans who wanted no deal regardless of the merits. When President Obama held out the possibility of limited uranium enrichment, it came with significant conditions. The Iranians would have to agree to far more rigorous inspections of their nuclear facilities than they'd ever countenanced before. If the offer had been made in a public forum, it would have been easy for the Iranians to create mischief by separating the inspections from the enrichment and accusing the president of making an offer he never intended to follow through on. In the safer sphere of secrecy, we could build momentum toward the broad outlines of a deal without committing to any single position. As the interim agreement specifically stated, "Nothing is agreed until everything is agreed."

Not least, confidentiality allowed the two teams to explore new ideas without exposing them to criticism from partisans in our respective countries who would be looking to sabotage any deal, no matter its merits. Ahmadinejad also benefited by keeping those on his left from making hay of the secret talks during a presidential election. In almost every respect, the back-channel talks had achieved precisely what we'd hoped.

◇◇◇◇◇◇◇◇◇◇◇◇

None of this made my present task any easier. I've learned that the best course in delicate situations is to say what needs to be said directly and promptly. As soon as I arrived in Brussels, I asked for a private meeting with Cathy Ashton. I wasn't too worried about how she would take it—Cathy is a consummate professional, an adult who knows the real world—and indeed she received the news with aplomb.

My fellow political directors took the revelation with what I would describe as fatalistic reserve. Our status as the superpower makes scenes like this one predictable, and even our allies can get frosty about it. Only occasionally did I experience real frustration from them. On occasion, when we'd disagree over some point, Helga Schmid would brusquely threaten to turn whatever task we were working on completely over to me. "You do it, Wendy," she'd bark, her eyes flashing as she went into Bavarian mode, sliding the files across the table toward me and crossing her arms. A moment later, her point made, we'd be colleagues again, both of us understanding that the EU's coordination role was essential to gaining the support from the international community that we all would need for any final deal.

The loudest complaint from my colleagues about the back channel was that I had nothing to show them on paper. As a group, we had exhibited amazing forbearance about leaking to the press, but the White House didn't want to risk that streak now by passing out the proposals in hard copies, one of which might find its way to the press. Instead, I briefed everyone fully on the terms and explained that, shortly after we broke up, the text of what we'd provisionally agreed on in Oman would be available for them at the American embassies in their capitals.

What none of them said was probably the hardest for them to swallow: they had to hear all this from me. On paper, I was one of them; by putting out the word about the back channel at our level, I had implicitly become first among equals. They were now in the position of reporting the news up their respective governments' chains of command, taking their cues from one of their own.

Let's just say that the luncheon that followed our meeting was less digestible than most of the meals I'd shared with that group.

◇◇◇◇◇◇◇◇◇◇

Two weeks later, the P5+1 representatives came to Geneva as planned, and the French exacted their revenge.

Both the Iranian and US teams arrived in Switzerland hoping the P5+1 group would, if not rubber-stamp, then approve at least the overall direction of the back-channel talks as the basis of a final agreement. More than that, we wanted to put a down payment of sorts on a permanent deal during our stay in Geneva. The P5+1 nations would make explicit the quite limited sanctions relief suggested in the provisional agreement—unfreezing some Iranian bank accounts, easing the ban on sales of some Iranian petroleum products, gold, and other commodities—in return for the freeze and even rollback of some of Iran's nuclear program. The political directors' meetings went well—so well that the Iranians leaked the news that John Kerry was on his way to Geneva to sign an interim agreement. Expecting a major breakthrough, the world press had gathered outside the hotel where we were meeting. The Russian foreign minister, Lavrov, had a bottle of champagne under his seat at the table. Back in Tehran, people stayed up into the night, glued to their televisions, to celebrate.

But French foreign minister Laurent Fabius was ready with a power play of his own. Hearing that Kerry was on his way, Fabius flew in first and went directly to the press on landing, pronouncing himself dissatisfied with the interim deal as it was written. Fabius said that he worried that the current terms were too easy on Iran. "One wants a deal," he said, "but not a sucker's deal."

To be quite fair, Fabius's move was more than payback for being kept in the dark over the past year. Early on, the French had appointed themselves the hard-liners among the P5+1 who would press for the most restrictive terms. In part, it was speculated, this stance was aimed at bolstering their relations with Iran's main rival, Saudi Arabia. The Saudis are a major supplier of oil to France, but more pertinently, a ready buyer of French military equipment.

No doubt, Fabius had genuine problems with the outline of the deal too. Our other European partners had similar concerns. Things had perhaps moved too quickly for their qualms to be settled in a fortnight. Of course, Fabius could have raised his objections in private, as the other ministers did. Instead, he had violated, in sensational fashion, our unspoken rule against speaking unilaterally to the press in advance of agreement to do so.

Whatever his exact calculations, Fabius's refusal infuriated Iran. The regime's unofficial voice, the Fars News Agency, cited the "destructive roles of France and Israel" (Israel is often thrown into any bad result for good measure), and President Rouhani made a speech saying that his country wouldn't be bullied. Those of us who had expected to come away from Geneva with a signed interim agreement in hand were none too pleased either.

Rather than blast Fabius, Secretary Kerry characteristically invited him to his hotel suite in Geneva to listen to his concerns. Fabius was worried that the interim agreement left too much room for Iran to claim a "right" to enrich uranium. He also wanted it to be clear that Iran could not continue construction on the Arak nuclear reactor it was building southwest of Tehran. Kerry then took Fabius's points back to the negotiating table, and, predictably, the Iranians balked. The status of the Arak reactor and claiming their due on enrichment were precious to them. And with that, the current deal we'd worked so hard on was off. Permanently? We didn't know. We agreed to reconvene two weeks later in the same place.

After the expectation of a historic announcement and the attendant hoopla, the foreign ministers departed, assuring the press, as usual, that the gap between the two sides was narrow.

Senator John McCain, a Republican who opposed the deal, cele-
brated by tweeting, "Vive La France."

◇◇◇◇◇◇◇◇◇◇◇◇

By the time we reassembled in Geneva in late November, we had
sat down with the Iranians bilaterally and also with the P5+1 and the
EU to accommodate Fabius's objections and those of others, all of
which were now attended to in the document. All of the P5+1 representatives signed on to the Joint Plan of Action in short order. The
interim agreement would pull back on a very few of the sanctions that
were tying up Iran's economy, furnish them with some US$7 billion
in Iranian funds that had been frozen in foreign banks, and suspend
bans on their auto industry and the trade in airplane parts so they
could upgrade debilitated airliners. Airplane malfunctions had already
caused many civilian deaths in Iran.

In return, Iran would deeply cut its production of enriched
uranium and allow international inspectors into its nuclear sites. The
plan was designed to build confidence in the Iranians' willingness and
ability to comply with a long-term deal and give the Iranian people a
taste of what that deal would mean, while we hammered out the final
details. We gave ourselves six months to finish.

What had been a sluggish and wayward trek through the bizarre
world of Iranian resentments and delays now became a rush to the
finish line. With the back channel closed out (though Bill and Jake
continued to be immensely helpful, never entirely exiting the negotiation), the P5+1 talks were now the sole carrier of our hopes, and as
the lead negotiator for the US team, I was the de facto leader of the
effort.

◇◇◇◇◇◇◇◇◇◇◇

Power comes naturally to some people. I don't think anyone who knew me as a teenager back in Baltimore would have picked me to be running a major nuclear arms deal thirty years later. My sister recalls me as a preteen homebody who liked to sit in her room and read. True, I had been named the girl most likely to succeed by my senior class in high school, based on my passion for social justice and politics that I'd inherited from my parents, but if you'd told me at the time that one day I'd be negotiating arms pacts with far-off Islamic clerics, I would have scoffed. More than that, I would have told you I didn't want to do it. Wearing the mantle of the power of the United States is not something I ever aspired to.

Luckily, since then, I've had wonderful role models who taught me how to understand power. One is my friend, former boss, and business partner, Madeleine Albright. Years ago, when she was serving as UN ambassador in the Clinton administration, Madeleine told me that the trick is not to simply wield your personal power, but to own the power of your office. Who, after all, can truly measure up to the outsized might of the United States? "When you sit across the negotiating table," Madeleine told me, "you are the United States of America, not Wendy. If you know that and use that, it matters more than the fact that you're a woman." Madeleine showed me that owning that power was quite something.

This isn't just true for ambassadors and cabinet secretaries. We all draw power from the roles we fill in life, whether we are acting as a parent or spouse, a boss or an employee. Every one of these roles comes with rights and responsibilities, as well as expectations about how to carry ourselves. Part of learning how to be a good parent or boss is learning to be firm but respectful. Part of being a good spouse is learning to be supportive and to demand support in return, as well as learning how the two of you, as a team, can be powerful.

This approach to assuming one's personal power made sense to me. I have never been afraid to stand up in public. As a young girl, I took creative acting classes on Saturdays. I enjoyed getting into other people's psyches. It imbued in me a sense of imagination and a better understanding of what it means to stand in another's shoes. I attribute my knack for adopting a role to being my father's daughter. His sense of living up to the important moment gave me an idea of how to rise to big occasions.

Former senator Barbara Mikulski showed me another way of owning my power. Barbara doesn't just assume a role—she transforms it by inhabiting it. Not even five feet tall and comfortably round, Barbara makes for an unlikely politician, as she acknowledged when running for the Senate in 1985. "I'm not particularly glamorous-looking," she said about her difficulty measuring up to her primary opponents, Representative Mike Barnes and Governor Harry Hughes, and flatly stated that "I just didn't look the part." Barbara had no hope of growing more "senatorial," saying, "I guess they don't make togas in size 14 petite."

She won anyway, and went on to serve longer than any woman in Congress. Her power came from being a hardworking and effective community organizer in immigrant neighborhoods in Baltimore. "That's what the voters wanted. They wanted someone...who looked like them, fought like them, talked like them and would stand up for them," she once told Ellen Malcolm of EMILY's List, as Ellen reported in her book with Craig Unger, *Why Women Win*. It didn't hurt, of course, that Barbara could talk in a steady stream of sound bites and had an intellect that always surprised.

Watching Barbara over the last forty years and more, I've seen that the powerful role you take on can eventually be—and should be—very close to the person you really are. You should change and grow in the role, but you can also change the way people think of the office you fill. Recalling how she was able to find her place in the male-dominated Senate in 1986 (there was only one other female senator when she arrived, Nancy Kassebaum), Barbara said that her attitude was, "This is what the part looks like and this is what the part is going to look like."

Mikulski's authenticity, her willingness to be who she was, made real the phrase "make the personal political." She turned her own experience in the ethnic, blue-collar sections of Baltimore into laws that benefited all Americans in need. She helped ensure that spouses could survive financially when their partner had high medical bills, as happened to her mom following her father's Alzheimer's diagnosis. She worked for the idea that women should get equal pay for equal work. Instead of wasting time trying to fulfill what other people thought a senator should look like, she made the office of US senator look like her.

◇◇◇◇◇◇◇◇◇◇

I've learned a lot from men wielding their power too, and I've greatly admired many of them. The question of how women use their power, however, is far more complicated, more difficult, and more urgent today than it is for men. Women, it must be said, have a strange relationship with power. We aren't afraid of it necessarily, but we seem more comfortable with informal power than institutional power. Early in my career, while organizing in local neighborhoods,

I did a study with another social work student, looking at the evolution of leadership in neighborhood organizations. Most often those organizations were started by women who, in order to protect their children, wanted the city to install a traffic light at a busy intersection, or worried about safe drinking water for their families. Women got busy and got the job done, without asking whether they could do so, when they could do something for someone else. As soon as their efforts had attracted the backing of grants and donors—that is, at the point that advocacy became an organization—men invariably stepped in. Whether elected or self-appointed, men became the head of the organization once the women had built it.

Perhaps this is why women are sometimes more comfortable working within a group. When I took on the job of Mikulski's chief of staff in the House, I found solace in a group of female chiefs of staff (or "administrative assistants," as both men and women were known then). Eleanor Lewis ran New York representative Gerry Ferraro's team. Nancy LeaMond was chief of staff for Mary Rose Oakar of Ohio. Nikki Heidepriem had led efforts on behalf of women's issues for the Democratic presidential campaign in 1984. Kitty Higgins worked for Michigan's Sandy Levin.

At our monthly Chinese take-out dinners in each other's homes, we talked about common issues and brainstormed better ways to do our jobs and manage our personal lives. This bunch of seasoned political aides sustained me when I was learning the job on the fly, constantly playing catch-up, and thinking sometimes that I was going to lose my mind.

But in those primitive days for women in the House, we did more than comfort one another. We proved, at least to each other, that it was possible to do our jobs and still live full lives and not go crazy. We talked each other through the rough spots and served as models for each other. It was only after I became pregnant with my daughter—I had told Barbara when she hired me that I hoped to have a child in the near future—that Nancy LeaMond felt that she could do the same. Just by being there, we established that we could be both women and chiefs of staff. In doing so, we changed each other and in ways large and small changed everyone's expectations about working in the House.

I would never give up the friendships I formed with those women. But looking back, I realize that we already had the skills to do our jobs before we started. We had the smarts to learn the ropes on our own. Women are often in denial about their own capabilities and search for others—groups of women or commanding men—to establish their power. When doing important personal work, like caring for our parents and children, the old and the young—both tasks that fall primarily to women—we are far more adept at adapting to new work and unfamiliar situations. When called on to make ends meet, we do what we must without stopping to doubt ourselves. Women excel at times when they have no choice but to take the job and do their best. Why can't we have the same confidence in the jobs we want and like as well? We may not always have the knowledge going in, but I'd trust any woman to figure out nearly any job.

Guys rarely question whether they can do the next job up. In my experience, they say yes and either worry about what they need to know later or—it's been known to happen—not at all. There is research that indicates this isn't just my own anecdotal observation. A widely cited internal study done by Hewlett-Packard in 2017 showed that men will apply for a job when they have 60 percent of the qualifications for the post; women will only do so when they can show that they have all of them.

It's an open question precisely why women continue to deny their own capabilities, despite the past century of feminist activism. We know that women are still told to be quiet, and that we are still interrupted when we don't comply. We know that men are told to push themselves forward while women are told to hang back. We worry when we are given more responsibility or more power, and too often we still believe that we don't know enough, aren't skilled enough, aren't substantive enough, to do what the job we are applying for requires. When I became the assistant secretary for legislative affairs at the State Department, I'd already run a congressional representative's office and a Senate campaign and served as executive director of both EMILY's List and the Democratic National Committee during a national presidential campaign (Mike Dukakis's). My résumé was among the most accomplished in Washington. Yet when the job was offered to me, I was completely overwhelmed by what I didn't know.

One way to address the confidence issue early is through all-women schools. I went to Smith because it was all women. Only women would raise their hands in class, only women would lead, only women would speak up. It was empowering and helped us to get ready for the "real" world. It is no accident that our most prominent female political leaders—Hillary Clinton, Madeleine Albright, Barbara Mikulski, and Nancy Pelosi—went to all-women colleges.

When we go out into the world, however, we are faced with the bias that our time in women's schools let us avoid and that we have no experience in combating. My field of national security and foreign policy has long been the domain of men. Although we have had three women secretaries of state, a glance at the major foreign policy publications and the panelists at major conferences will show that our security and diplomacy leaders are still predominantly men.

It is not our numbers alone that put us at a disadvantage. As undersecretary of state for political affairs, I often attended meetings in the White House Situation Room, the underground, secure conference room where senior policymakers debate the government's way forward, often with the president in the room to finalize the decisions being made. At the time the top positions on the National Security Council were all occupied by women, with Susan Rice as national security adviser and Avril Haines and Lisa Monaco as her deputies. These amazingly talented women, then all in their forties, gave away nothing to male staffers in the depth of their analysis or their ability to articulate it.

Yet even in this environment, men's voices were heard differently than the women's. As we went around the table giving our views on the topic of the day, one of the women would make a point. After one or two speakers had followed with further comments, a male at the table would inevitably repeat nearly verbatim the point made by Susan, Avril, Lisa, or me. To my amazement, no one would remark that the point had already been made; rather, they would affirm their male colleague's statement by saying, "Good point."

Soon a quiet realization dawned on us: we girls had to stick together. The women of the Situation Room developed an unspoken rule. When any man commented by repeating something that had been said earlier by a woman, one of the other women at the table would jump in. "I'm glad you agree with what ——— just said," one of us would say about our female colleague's identical comment, or else, "That builds nicely on the point ——— made just before." We tried to be subtle—so subtle sometimes that I'm not convinced it always penetrated the consciousnesses of the men in the room. But we did what we could to make sure we were heard, affirmed, and acknowledged, which was a wonderfully empowering experience.

I try to do something similar when I do speaking engagements. After I've finished my prepared remarks, I customarily open the floor to questions. The first questioner is almost always a man, usually followed by another man. If by the fourth question no women have raised their hands, I stop the question period and say that I won't continue until I hear from some of the women in the room. That brings nervous laughter, recognition, and finally some raised hands from women.

The real drawback of this dynamic is that it affects how women do their jobs. When Madeleine Albright became the first female secretary of state, she understood that her first task was to assure people that she was strong enough to do the job. So she asked President Clinton to nominate Strobe Talbott, Tom Pickering, Stu Eizenstat, and Tim Wirth as her deputy and key undersecretaries. Rather than an admission that she needed men's help, appointing men to these spots sent the message that she could handle, and even welcome, their strength. It must have been incredibly frustrating to constantly have to prove her ease with the role she was so clearly cut out for. For her closest staff, she hired women who could be counted on for a straightforward chat when she needed to get her thoughts in order—Elaine Shocas to be her chief of staff, with Suzy George as deputy CoS. Along with me as her counselor, Madeleine always had a travel companion with whom she could talk directly about her own use of power or, if needed, whether she needed to reapply her lipstick.

Madeleine also had to take care to show that she was willing to fight. Not a warmonger by any stretch of the imagination, she did understand that women are perceived as hesitant to use force. As UN ambassador, she had burnished her credentials when she traveled with the chairman of the Joint Chiefs, General John Shalikashvili, to peacekeeping missions. When she became secretary, her approach to the conflict in Kosovo was so adept that *Time* magazine put her on the cover with the line, "Madeleine's War."

When I consider how Madeleine managed to change the way we think of women in power, I see that she did it by embracing her femininity, by never falling into the trap of acting like a man to claim equality with men. Madeleine loves clothes and chooses what she wears with care. From her trademark brooches that she used to make diplomatic points to her impeccable style of dress and her love of popular culture, she didn't allow the role of secretary of state to change the fact that she was a woman.

Madeleine's interpretation of an independent woman in executive power set a standard that hadn't been updated since Geraldine Ferraro's turn as the Democratic vice presidential candidate in 1984. The evening Gerry was nominated, I was on the floor of the convention. Every woman working on the campaign somehow found her way to the floor that night. It was an electric, extraordinary moment. Yet the image-making that surrounded this leap forward was the truer indicator of where women were at. When Walter Mondale announced her as his running mate, Gerry appeared wearing a white dress— America could handle a woman acceding to power, but only, her outfit shouted, if she came off as demure and virginal, looking like she was about to walk down the aisle, not be nominated for vice president of the United States.

By the time Hillary Clinton appeared onstage at the Democratic convention to accept the nomination for president, thirty-two years later, she too wore white, but times had changed. Her choice to wear white was a bold one, an echo of the white dresses of suffragettes who'd demonstrated in favor of the women's vote a century before. And she wore a white pantsuit, one like the black ones she took to wearing when she'd run for the Senate so she wouldn't have to worry about choosing an outfit each day and so the press would stop writing about her appearance. I truly believe that the difference in the perceptions of her white pantsuit and of Gerry's white dress had a lot to do with how Madeleine changed the discussion in the interim.

Hillary owed her pantsuits, however, to Barbara Mikulski. When she ran for Senate, Barbara had a dressmaker fit her out with skirt suits in solid colors, which made up a little for her shortness. She also had the dressmaker sew an inside pocket in the jacket so that, like guys, she could store a speech or notecards and a lipstick without having to carry a pocketbook on the campaign trail. Once she was elected, however, Barbara wanted more options, particularly on cold, winter days. She went to see Robert Byrd, the Senate majority leader and a tradition-keeper for the chamber, seeking his permission to wear pants. She succeeded, endearing herself to all the women staffers in the Senate and changing the look on the floor forever.

The optics may have changed, but what happens to women who seek power has not. Geraldine Ferraro was a seasoned member of Congress from Queens who had an ease with the press and a realistic sense of people's day-to-day lives, yet she took a beating over her husband's business dealings, which came to define her in a way that no male politician has been judged by his wife's business, taxes, or finances. A woman who doesn't marry can answer for her own choices, not for her husband. Barbara Mikulski's lack of a publicly identified male companion opened the way for her opponent in her

Senate run, Republican congresswoman Linda Chavez, to call her a "San Francisco Democrat."

With all these competing pressures, it's no wonder that women arrive in the halls of power determined to outdo everyone, overachieve, and outrun the negative assumptions. When Hillary Clinton came to the US Senate in 2000, she put her head down, worked like a dog, and gained bipartisan respect for doing her homework. She strove to know as much as anyone else in the room about the issues and represented New Yorkers with strength and effectiveness. As secretary of state, she reinstated US diplomacy on the world stage by applying her immense skill and left with historic approval ratings.

Because women leaders have to be better prepared and more on top of their game to succeed, we also can easily become micromanagers. During her Senate campaign, we made Barbara agree to spend her time being the candidate and skip weekly evening campaign strategy meetings with her team of advisers, letting go of control, which did not come easily for her. For Hillary, knowing more about the subject at hand than anyone else became a negative in her run for president, as voters focused more on the big picture than on her preparation, and on her personality rather than her ability to get the job done. In her effort to be acceptable, Hillary may inadvertently have diminished her own stature as the first woman to have a credible shot at the office.

Most of us won't ever feel the sting of losing the presidency because we're women. It's easy to dismiss more casual, workaday examples of the diminishment of women's power as minor annoyances, the kind of jostling that can be found whenever men and women come together. As a group of us were sorting out last details on the eve of announcing the final agreement in Vienna in 2015, some of the foreign ministers who had already arrived in town went to dinner with a few aides. It so happened that, because of the extraordinary composition of the P5+1 team, those of us still leading the work were mostly women. As we worked to get to closure on the last details of the agreement, text messages began to transmit back to some of us that some ministers were making derogatory jokes about how much more efficient the process would be if men were in charge. Helga and I agreed not to get distracted by the misogyny and just get the work done.

Women have lived inside these clichés for so long that we can lose the energy to fight them, and worse, sometimes we adopt them ourselves. In 2011, when news came that Bill Burns was going to be named deputy secretary of state under Secretary Clinton, I called Cheryl Mills, Hillary's chief of staff, to let her know I was interested in replacing Bill as undersecretary for political affairs. Cheryl and I had some initial conversations that seemed to indicate I was being considered. Then things went silent. In Washington, interviewing for a major position is a bit of a blood sport. Reporters and pundits kick around names quite publicly, so success or failure is never a private matter. If I was going to be passed over, I wondered whether it was better that my name had fallen off the roster early. In any case, there was nothing further to be done.

Some weeks later, Cheryl called to say I was back under consideration. Would I meet her for a Sunday breakfast to discuss?

When we met, Cheryl explained that the secretary was disposed favorably toward me, but that a concern had been raised about me that I was not a team player and thus wouldn't be a good fit. I strained to figure out where this was coming from. I thought perhaps it emanated from when I had been assistant secretary of legislative affairs, a post that required me to tell powerful people in the State Department that their priority was not the president's and thus, they could not go up to Capitol Hill to push for their own agendas. It was hard to imagine that I'd be faulted years afterward for doing what was only my job. As we talked, however, it became clear that "not a team player" really meant "too assertive."

I was stunned. Throughout my career, I'd been called "tough." It was a compliment that was regularly paid to women in Washington who demanded excellent work, but of course, it always sounded less begrudging when it was said of a man. In the competition for the political affairs job, "tough" had somehow become "too assertive." Critiques like this one, along with being called "ambitious" or "aggressive," are often lodged against women. They had been lodged against Secretary Clinton and Cheryl herself. Indeed, I was dismayed that these two very strong and powerful women believed about me the very unfair criticisms that had been pointed at them. Cheryl said she would get back to me. Finally, an evening meeting was set up at Secretary Clinton's home in Washington. Hillary and I talked about the job itself and my ideas for how to do it, but eventually she brought up some of the same questions Cheryl had. She respected me enough to be direct with me about what she'd heard, and I answered with the same honesty, repeating what I'd told Cheryl. I left still not knowing if an offer would come.

In Washington, no advocate is more valuable than the person who did the job before you, and did it well. Bill Burns, with whom I had worked closely during the Clinton presidency, was one of my champions inside the department. He stepped in, telling the secretary that I would be a great team player. In the end, Secretary Clinton, with President Obama's agreement, nominated me to the post, and I became the first woman undersecretary of state for political affairs.

The experience showed me how pervasive the culture's attitudes toward women are: here were two powerful women who had both fought against such stereotypes themselves but who couldn't decode what they'd heard about me as similarly putting another woman in a box. I was surprised, but I shouldn't have been. When I thought about it, I realized that I'd done the same to my own mother.

When I lost my mother very suddenly twelve years ago, I was stunned when I walked into the funeral home for her service and saw that the place was packed with hundreds of mourners. Mom was eighty-one when she died, old enough that many of her friends had passed away or moved away. My father was a beloved local business-man who had given many Baltimoreans a job and then went on to bravely take on the racial status quo. I would not have been surprised if all of these people had come to his funeral (and indeed, five years later his funeral was equally well attended). Yet in addition to plenty of people Mom's own age, here were middle-aged men and women and a sprinkling of younger folks. My image of my mother was, to my discredit, not in line with reality. Yes, she had primarily been a home-maker who supported our family as we went out into the world. I often said, "Mom would have been something else had she been born a decade later."

I've come to realize that Mom was indeed something else. She had attended community college in Baltimore County even as she raised the three of us kids. When she and my father moved to Atlanta, she started her own real estate career, and when they returned to Mary-land she kept it going. By the time she died, she was considered the "Condo Queen" of Baltimore and was a mentor to many younger col-leagues. As her own role had expanded from wife and mother to in-clude businesswoman, she had found her own sense of self and power. I had missed that change because I saw her in terms of what I needed from her—a nurturing mom—and no doubt also because, although times were changing, I grew up steeped in a culture that was most comfortable with women who tended to the home while men went out and worked. We all get used to overlooking women's contributions inside and outside the home. This puts women in a double bind. If we trumpet our accomplishments, we look too ambitious and pushy. If we hang back, we look as if we lack confidence. Either way, we pay a price—usually watching others take credit for what we've done. Worse yet, when we make an effort to be recognized, our demand to be valued isn't enough—men have to validate us, as Bill did for me, or else other, more powerful women have to intervene.

A relatively recent experience is an example of how complicated it can get. After I'd left government and was working in the private sector, a woman I worked with came to see me one day. She ran operations for the company, and because hers was a support role, she had only occasional contact with the company's clients. But as she correctly pointed out, every client relationship completely depended on her performing at a high level. She felt that the partners did not appreciate her contribution and would never make her one of them. I knew the partners well and agreed that they might be reluctant. Their reluctance, however, shouldn't be an excuse for not owning her own power, I argued. I suggested that she approach each partner personally to make her case.

My colleague agreed that, at the very least, she should approach each partner and take the time to explain why she felt she was due the title and extra compensation of a partner. We outlined her case, and she practiced her pitch with another female colleague. Even if she didn't succeed, she'd feel that she had made her best effort and at the very least laid the foundation for the future. Her self-empowerment itself, she felt, would be worth it.

Her pitch to the partners went well, and she convinced several of the members of the partnership committee. But her assertiveness carried her only part of the way. After my colleague made her rounds to argue for herself, the committee signaled that they would elevate three new partners—all of them men. At this, the senior woman partner at the firm put her foot down. She would vote yes on the three men, but only if a comparable woman was elevated in their partner class. With support from some of the male partners, she at last convinced the committee to include my colleague in the new partner class.

More women need to stand up for each other as this senior partner did. No tale in Washington about women moving up is as telling as how Madeleine Albright got to be secretary of state in the first place. As her name came up as a possibility, she urged those of us who backed her not to make her the "women's" candidate. She wanted, as most of us do, to be considered on her merits. However, as various press stories put her name on the short list, the *Washington Post* quoted White House sources calling Madeleine "second tier." Furious, the women around Madeleine went to work placing strategic calls to the first lady and to Vice President Al Gore to boost her chances, while talking to our contacts in the press to make the argument off the record that the talk of Madeleine's being "second tier" was pure sexism. This maelstrom, with Hillary's urging clinching the deal, convinced President Clinton to make the historic decision to put Madeleine forward.

I've always made it a rule to take any call or answer any email from a young woman looking for guidance; I help a lot of young men as well, but women are my priority, because I have watched how well the boys' network operates. In many places, but especially in Washington, there is a tight cadre of guys in national security and foreign policy who recommend each other on a consistent basis for every good job that comes along. We women need to do the same for each other and insist that the boys' network consider capable women as well when those jobs come along.

More than anything, women have to become more accustomed to getting power. And we need to recognize the power we already possess. At one point, I got an email from a former colleague, a young career professional who had worked with me at the State Department and had taken a job in the New York State government in order to be closer to family. She had always had a deep passion for advocacy on behalf of women and families and was now looking to make another career shift. In her initial email, she asked me how best to position herself to land a job with a national advocacy organization. She hoped that I could introduce her to leaders and help her build out her network.

But my former colleague had buried the lead in her request. She already had the entrée she needed. She could call anyone in America, or around the world for that matter, on behalf of New York State. Since Seneca Falls, the birthplace of women's rights, was in New York, she had the perfect platform for talking about advancing women's issues. Doing the job she had, and doing it well, was the best path to fulfilling her interests. She had the power; she needed to own it and use it to serve New York and at the same time serve her own ambition. A year later, that is exactly what she had done.

Women need to stop thinking that "power" is a dirty word, or that the trappings of power matter less than the work. When President Clinton and Secretary Albright asked me to come back to government as Madeleine's counselor, I asked to be confirmed with the rank of ambassador. It was one of the smartest things I ever asked for. I knew that as a woman and without line authority, I needed some heft beyond the position, and so the Senate confirmed me as an ambassador. It has been immensely helpful. When, in that position, I led American delegations to, for instance, trilateral talks with Japan and South Korea on North Korea and all the delegations were men, being "Ambassador Sherman" undoubtedly helped when I dealt with North Korea. The title has been helpful ever since.

Women have a tremendous amount of power that comes with the roles we play in society, far more power than we ever had before. We cannot wield this power positively without understanding our strengths and owning them. At the same time, we have to appreciate that so many of the remaining obstacles to women's advancement—most blatantly, perhaps, the sexual harassment in the workplace that has become an important topic of conversation—are all about power. We must each have the courage to stand up for what is right. We also need to rediscover the power of working collectively and become adept at using social media to speak with one voice. The challenge for many of us remains the interpersonal moments, when we have to risk being called tough, aggressive, even difficult. Our only response must be to continue to view—and use—power positively.

chapter four

LETTING GO

In the late winter of 1981, I was in my office at Maryland's Child Welfare Agency in Baltimore when my phone rang. It was my mother calling from Atlanta, where she and my father had moved some years before so my father could take a job with a large real estate company. It was unusual for Mom to call me at work, and in the time it took her to draw a breath before she spoke, I knew something was wrong. I also somehow knew that it was about my brother, Doug.

Seven years my junior, Doug was gorgeous, intense, funny, and very lost. Since leaving the University of Georgia at Athens a couple of years before, he had been making his life in Atlanta, working with my dad a little on land sales. The previous year he'd gotten married to Beth, a lovely local woman he'd met at school. My husband and I had come down for the wedding on St. Simons Island, a beautiful spot off Georgia's coast. It was great to see Doug looking at home among his new in-laws, in part because, until then, he'd never seemed to fit into southern culture.

Now, trying to hold herself together on the phone, my mother explained that the night before Doug had taken Beth's gun and driven off in his car. There had been no argument, no precipitating event. He had left without saying good-bye. Sometime in the early morning, he'd pulled off the highway at a rest stop some miles from Atlanta and ended his life.

I don't remember much of what I said then. I could hardly breathe. I do know that I told my mother I would be on the next plane to Atlanta. After I hung up, I explained to my assistant what had happened and told her I'd be away for a few days. A colleague followed me in her car to make sure I got home all right.

Home was a tidily renovated row house in an up-and-coming part of Baltimore, a symbol of my new grown-up life. At thirty-one, I had a serious, demanding job and a house of my own, and after surviving a divorce, I was married to Bruce Stokes, a wonderful man. But at this moment my life felt strangely alien, like a shell containing me, another shell.

The shock of Doug's death was all the more horrifying because it didn't come as a surprise. As a kid growing up, he'd fit in well with our tight-knit, mostly Jewish suburb outside Baltimore. He spent much of his time among the large, roving group of neighborhood boys. His problems began just as he was hitting adolescence, when he left this sheltered existence. My father, watching his real estate business slowly founder because of his civil rights activism, had taken a job as head of marketing and sales with Jim Rouse, a legendary Maryland real estate developer who was laying out an idyllic planned community west of Baltimore and north of Washington called Columbia.

Rouse was a visionary who is best known for his part in remodeling Boston's 150-year-old landmark Faneuil Hall into a cluster of shops and restaurants, thereby inventing the modern urban marketplace. Rouse also created some of the first suburban shopping malls.

But he was also a devout Christian who had advocated for urban renewal before the term even existed. He had cofounded the affordable housing nonprofit Baltimore Neighborhoods, through which he had come to know my father and supported his integration efforts. In Columbia, Rouse pictured an open and integrated community. He wanted it to be different from the cookie-cutter subdevelopments that had begun to encircle Baltimore and Washington in the 1960s.

Rouse believed that a town laid out on progressive principles could foster a good life. His idea of what that meant sounds modern even today. Columbia would respect the natural shape of the 15,000 acres of former farmland. It would mix low-lying, higher-density apartments with traditional suburban ranches. He seeded the town with small office parks so residents could work as well as live in the area. And unlike the typical white-flight suburb, Columbia would combine affordable apartments and houses with market-priced ones and arrange all these options around village centers to keep the place economically and racially integrated.

Working to realize Rouse's ideal town was the perfect outlet for Dad's experience and passion. My parents pulled up stakes and built an open-plan contemporary home on a lakefront lot in Columbia. They were proud to be Columbia pioneers, among the town's first citizens.

But in this idealized existence, Doug struggled. The schools, like everything else about the place, were progressive. The open classrooms and unstructured days didn't suit Doug's style of learning. The streets were safe and pleasant, but Columbia was not a homogenous, supportive community like Pikesville, where Doug had thrived. He seemed to lose his shape, and possibly to shore himself up, he started taking drugs. Halfway through what was shaping up as a desultory

high school career, Doug and some of his friends were caught breaking into a pharmacy back in his old neighborhood.

After that, on the advice of a counselor, my parents sent Doug to
a boarding school in New Hampshire in hopes that a change of scene
and more academic discipline would make a difference. He did well
enough to graduate and get into college at the University of Georgia,
but we suspected that his drug habit had continued.

We also knew that Doug's difficulties were more than delinquency
or a fondness for drugs and alcohol. Depression ran in my father's family: his sister and father had both committed suicide, and Dad, though
you'd never suspect it of such an upbeat, motivated man, had been
taking antidepressants for years. Doug was seeing a psychiatrist at the
time of his death, but we knew so much less about depression and
drug addiction than we do now. Had we known more, my family might
have had a better chance of helping him. We'd have recognized earlier
that Doug's illicit drug habits were his attempt at self-medicating.

Even then, however, we did have a sense that his personal problems and his mental health were related. Doug had been in a bad
auto accident while he was at the University of Georgia. It came out
later that he'd been high on cocaine, and that drugs had probably
caused the crash. Within the family, we wondered whether Doug had
been looking for a way out.

If he was, his near-miss only made things worse. He spent weeks in
intensive care, followed by a long rehabilitation. He had traumatic brain
injury (about which we also knew less back in those days) and suffered
short-term-memory problems, which complicated his ability to work.

For a while, not long before his death, things seemed to be looking up for him. He was taking courses at Georgia State, and he
started seeing his psychiatrist. My father let Doug help out with the

real estate deals he was working on. When he married Beth, a sweet woman from a gracious Georgia family, we thought—hoped—that he'd found his way.

But he never did regain his footing. In a miserable irony, Doug, who had always been uncomfortable with the gun-loving side of southern culture, took his life with Beth's pistol.

Were we surprised, then, by Doug's death? It would be nonsensical to say yes. But the devastating loss of our brother and son was not the only shock we were dealing with. The violation of a sense of order in our lives came like a hammer blow and was completely unexpected. I remember with acute clarity flying down to Atlanta, dreading the days ahead. First would be the funeral, of course, but that would take place quickly, as is the Jewish tradition. What I feared more was the overwhelming loss that, I knew even in those first days, would hang over me forever. We were all angry at Doug for killing himself, even as we mourned his life filled with a pain so terrible that he'd do anything to end it. And I was dealing with my own feeling of failure. I was a social worker, a mental health professional. Couldn't I have done more for him?

I wasn't alone. My family members all searched for something to blame, a way to think we could have affected what happened. An autopsy, required in Georgia when someone commits suicide in a public place, showed that Doug had no drugs or alcohol in his system when he took his life. That required us to face the fact of his suffering. My sister simply denied the reality at first. She couldn't believe that Doug had turned the gun on himself. Perhaps, she thought, someone had killed him.

No matter the circumstances, a death that close imparts an unexpected message: there are bigger things than you. Death challenges our human need to believe that we are in control of our lives, that we can and do affect those around us.

These days we are taught to understand intellectually that we are not in control. That message is in all our self-help books. We see it on motivational posters, hear it in the Serenity Prayer—"God grant me the serenity to accept those things I cannot change." It was a truism of my job. As the director of Maryland's Child Welfare Agency, I was responsible for thousands of cases of child abuse, foster care placements, adoptions, and children and teens in institutional care. I dealt daily with people who were coping with crisis. Most of them never expected the bounces their lives had taken.

We rarely experience our own path as anything but the result of our own decisions, good or bad. But I knew I was lucky to have my job, a new position the state had created that put a huge amount of responsibility on one person's shoulders. I had the sense to recognize how crazy it was to put a thirty-year-old barely out of graduate school in that job, but at the same time I felt I could do it. I had been confident in my ability to conquer whatever life threw at me. Now I wasn't so sure. For a consummate organizer like me, death's irreversibility—its non-negotiability—robbed me of my mistaken belief that any obstacle can be gotten around, bulldozed, or appealed to.

Besides the gut punch of my brother's suicide, I was worried about my future. I was stunned that depression had now announced itself in a third generation of Shermans. After my father's sister killed herself, my grandmother, having lost her daughter and her husband to suicide, had taken to asking aloud, "Who in this generation will it be?" I had to face the possibility that my still-hoped-for child would be vulnerable to depression. How would I tell him or her about the risks inherent in this family script? I began to see a therapist to help me through Doug's death, but also to sort out the question of whether I ought to have children at all. Eventually Bruce and I were blessed to have Sarah. As she got older, I told her that, given our family history, she needed to be vigilant about the symptoms of depression, just as someone genetically susceptible to heart disease or diabetes would watch out for symptoms of those diseases.

Every family, every life, has its tragedies—death or divorce or changed circumstances that brook no control and scramble the future. To the overachieving woman I was at the time, though, Doug's death brought home the profound lesson that comes from experiencing any deep loss. The world doesn't follow the script you've written for yourself.

In diplomacy, we always have to be prepared to accept our lack of control over circumstances. The world can and often will wreak havoc on our plans. The Middle East is a ready example. No diplomatic effort has seen as many failures, so many unscripted roadblocks and seeming dead ends, as the quest for peace in the Middle East. Even when we've had success—Jimmy Carter's Camp David accords and the Oslo Accords—tragedy and more disarray seem to follow.

Nonetheless, every American president seems to enter office pledging a fresh start or promising to pursue a groundbreaking new angle on solving the conflict. When I began at the State Department as assistant secretary for legislative affairs in the first months of the Clinton administration, the mood was cautiously upbeat. Secret negotiations sponsored by Norway had been going on in Oslo since the election that had put Clinton in office. Before he had been in an office a year, and before he had time to put his own ideas into circulation, President Clinton stood between Palestinian leader Yasser Arafat and Israeli prime minister Yitzhak Rabin on the White

House lawn, gently prodding the two to shake hands over the peace agreement they had just signed based on the Oslo Accords.

The document the two leaders signed that day, the Declaration of Principles on Interim Self-Government Arrangements, was less a true settlement than a hopeful new beginning for Middle East peace. The declaration stipulated that Israel would recognize the power of the Palestine Liberation Organization, which would become the Palestinian National Authority, to establish an interim government to administer the land their people occupied. In return, the PLO recognized the state of Israel and vowed to keep order and suppress attacks on their neighbor. This land-for-security swap has formed the framework of the peace process ever since.

But what was signed that day on the South Lawn was only a framework for peace. It detailed a series of show-me steps intended to build confidence on both sides. It laid out a schedule of Israeli troop withdrawals from Palestinian-claimed territory (minus, crucially, Jerusalem and the existing Israeli settlements). The Palestinian Authority would create a police force that could ensure security in the West Bank and Gaza and credibly patrol the borders with Jordan and Egypt. By the time negotiations ended seven years later with a final status agreement, both sides would have come to believe that the two-state solution enshrined in the Oslo Accords would work.

Or so we all thought. Confidence-building measures are a worthwhile approach to fashioning a deal when the conditions are right. They worked beautifully in the period between the interim nuclear agreement with Iran in November 2013 and the final agreement in July 2015 because both sides almost immediately saw the tangible benefits of the interim deal. Iran got some of its cash that had been sequestered in Western banks since the revolution, as well as much-needed airplane parts; the P5+1 side, meanwhile, could see that hundreds of Iran's centrifuges were being taken out of commission. The Oslo Accords' confidence-building steps turned out to be slower in coming, if they came at all. The confidence-building steps themselves depended on a minimum level of trust before either side was willing to take them.

Nonetheless, as I watched Arafat and Rabin clasp hands from my seat on the South Lawn, I felt as if I was watching a historic moment. It looked much like the famous handshake fourteen years earlier between Egyptian president Anwar Sadat and the prime minister of Israel, Menachem Begin, as President Jimmy Carter looked on. I will always remember that day as a bright blue sky, matching our bright hope for peace. But of course, in the end, Rabin and Arafat's handshake represented nothing so substantial.

President Clinton pursued his own Middle East agenda on top of the Oslo process, and for a while peace seemed to be breaking out all over. In October 1994, I watched King Hussein and Rabin sign the Israel-Jordan peace agreement in the Jordanian city of Aqaba on a day so excruciatingly hot that Clinton could barely read his remarks as sweat dripped suntan lotion into his burning eyes. The president also tried to foster agreements between Israel and Syria and between Israel and Lebanon, hoping to isolate Iran, which even then was backing worrisome elements in those Middle East nations.

But progress on the Oslo Accords was excruciatingly slow. Both Arafat and Rabin faced increasing dissent about taking the interim steps that Oslo mandated.

Protests turned into street violence, and not only the nagging disruptions from the Palestinian side that Oslo was designed to end. On November 4, 1995, Prime Minister Rabin, speaking at a peace rally in Kings of Israel Square in Tel Aviv, was assassinated by a twenty-five-year-old Israeli man, a radical right-winger who was opposed to peace with the Palestinians in general and withdrawal from the West Bank in particular.

Rabin's assassination was devastating for all who had hoped for peace. Not only was Rabin pushing his own people toward the settlement imagined in the Oslo deal, but he was a chief pillar of support for Arafat too. The PLO chief's leadership skills had always leant themselves better to resistance than nation-building. Rabin knew that he had to shore up his adversary as a partner for peace. It soon became clear that, without Rabin, Arafat would not be able to stand his ground against the hard-liners in the PLO.

Rabin's funeral, then, was something of a funeral for the Oslo process as well. The gathering of world leaders in Jerusalem for Rabin's rites just two days after his assassination became an un- expected moment of coming together in the wake of the tragedy. It prompted the first visit to Israel for President Hosni Mubarak of Egypt, the first public trip to Israel for King Hussein of Jordan, and a rare trip abroad for the chairman of the Senate Foreign Relations Committee, North Carolina senator Jesse Helms.

This was an odd moment for me. As State's liaison to Congress, it fell to me to escort a planeload of senators and representatives attending Rabin's funeral on an overnight military flight. Helms slept in the seat that most resembled a bed, Connecticut senator Chris Dodd took another chair, and the White House legislative affairs chief Pat Griffin and I took turns on the floor. Politics made strange bedfellows—this time quite literally.

The funeral was scheduled so quickly—again, following Jewish tradition—that the dignitaries hardly had time to absorb the profound sorrow of the occasion before their arrival. The feelings on display were still raw. Emotional speeches by President Clinton and King Hussein of Jordan were more than matched by Rabin's granddaughter. Afterward, the assembled dignitaries headed to the King David Hotel for the Jewish mourning ritual of *shiva*. As we approached the hotel's patio overlooking the city wall of Jerusalem, where all of Jewish history seems written, we came upon King Hussein, sitting alone, clearly contemplating all that had come before—the assassination of his father by an Arab, the half-century of hope and strife since, and now Rabin's murder by a citizen of his own country. "I've never been used to standing except with you next to me," Hussein had said at the funeral, addressing Rabin, "speaking about peace, speaking about our hopes and dreams of generations to come."

On the patio at the King David, the crowd of us all stopped as one person when we saw Hussein. Somehow it felt as if we all understood that we needed to give this man his time for reflection, if only for a few moments, to honor all he'd been through.

In 1996, I left the State Department, but the following year Madeleine Albright was named secretary of state for President Clinton's second term, and she invited me back as counselor. This position has a history going back to the early 1900s, when it was a position for the secretary's top adviser. Other secretaries have employed counselors as managers of special projects. I had no particular portfolio when I came on board, but did whatever Madeleine needed, often staying by her side as she tended to President Clinton's priorities around the globe.

One of those priorities was to bring the parties together to try to make the Oslo principles stick. Until that time, President Clinton had mostly been a facilitator of the Oslo process. Now, with his agenda mired in the investigation that would end in his impeachment, he

decided to take a central role in trying to solve the dilemma of getting
the Israelis and Palestinians moving toward fulfilling the plan. An initial sit-down was planned for October 1998. To help the president get
to as many sessions as possible, we hosted them at a conference center on the Wye River on the Eastern Shore of Maryland owned by the
Aspen Institute, the leadership and public affairs organization.

The meeting's bucolic backdrop—a one-thousand-acre former
plantation on the Chesapeake Bay—was supposed to induce a relaxed
spirit for the talks. But from the first moments after we arrived, the
mood was intense. Expected to span a long weekend, the Wye River
summit went on for eight difficult days, six of them with President
Clinton in attendance, and including one twenty-one-hour marathon.
Both sides pulled out all the stops. One morning, pretending to be fed
up and ready to leave, the Israelis put all of their suitcases out in front
of their lodgings, as if they were heading to the airport. On a hunch,
we sent an aide over to pick up one of the suitcases. It was empty, as
were all of them. We called their bluff and the negotiations continued.

We realized in the course of the talks that it was the step-by-step
approach of Oslo that was bogging the process down, but we couldn't
tackle a complete restructuring of the deal. All we could offer was to
break the steps down into specific, achievable goals and exhort the
two parties to take the risks involved. This is often the best way forward when a process has stalled and little in the way of courage or
creative problem-solving is on display: reaffirm the process.

Unfortunately, our promptings seemed to lead to more cautious
hedging. President Clinton decided that what was needed was a jolt.
As the talks wore on, the president wisely invited King Hussein to the
summit to instill sobriety and purpose in the proceedings. When the
king entered the room where negotiations were going on, everyone,

including Arafat and Benjamin Netanyahu (Rabin's successor as prime minister), was instantly hushed. Terminally ill with cancer, Hussein, who had spent his life pursuing peace in the Middle East, impressed upon everyone that time was short and peace necessary.

Hussein's appearance was a rare moment when the weight of history was brought to bear on a negotiation characterized by mistrust and dramatics that threatened to blow up the agreement. At the last minute, Prime Minister Netanyahu made a play to gain the release of Jonathan Pollard, a US sailor who was serving life in prison for spying for Israel, and a cause célèbre for many Israelis and American Jews. As we were finalizing the Wye River Memorandum, the formal document of what had been agreed, Netanyahu insisted that President Clinton had told him that the final agreement would include Pollard's release. Clinton was adamant that he'd made no such promise. Faced with walking away from the hard-fought session with nothing to show for it, Netanyahu folded, and soon after this dustup the parties flew by helicopters back to the White House for a ceremony.

In the months following, we tried to capitalize on Wye River's momentum, but the objections to Oslo continued to wear down all the parties involved. President Clinton refused to quit, however, convening the Israelis and Palestinians again in the summer of 2000 at Camp David, and twice more before the end of his presidency. A final conference at Taba, on the Sinai Peninsula, was held at his bequest, though it took place after he left office. Arafat could not get to yes. Two weeks later, in an Israeli election that was in part a referendum on the peace process, Ariel Sharon, a hard-liner who was not likely to allow Israeli-occupied land to be traded even for guarantees of a safer, more secure Israel, was voted in as prime minister. Peace in the Middle East, at least for the time being, was lost.

When you've been working hard to make the world safer, less violent, and more understanding, it's a devastating feeling to have a door shut in your face just as you think it's within reach. We diplomats live in denial—we never quite believe that the door has closed for good. We are eternal optimists, continuing to bring groups together or shuttling from one to the other, even as those looking on can see that nothing is going to change.

But diplomats can be haunted by the what-ifs years after the world has moved on.

These are times when it's important to remember that we are human and that even those of us who represent a superpower don't control everything.

Failure in diplomacy can sometimes be attributed to a lack of what I call "ripeness." In Shakespeare's *King Lear,* Edgar tells his co-conspirator Gloucester that he can't choose the time of his death any more than he could have chosen when he was born. "Ripeness is all," says Edgar.

The term has been adopted by the legal world to mean a situation that can't be resolved. A judge may refuse to rule on a case because, in his view, an event that will affect his decision has yet to play out. In a classic ripeness case, a company was not allowed to argue that a government regulation was unfair because the regulation hadn't yet gone into effect.

In diplomacy, ripeness is an agreement that can only be made when all of the parties have come to terms with what is needed—in this case, the need for peace. After the failure of Camp David, I had to console myself with the possibility that even had Rabin lived, Arafat might never have transformed himself and gone from being the leader of a resistance movement to the leader of a nation. That turn of history, or that turn in his character, had not yet arrived on the world stage, a fact that no amount of diplomatic skill was going to change.

◇◇◇◇◇◇◇◇◇◇◇

If the pain of letting a deal get away is proportional to how close you get to completing it, the hardest failure I've ever had to accept is the long-range missile test moratorium with North Korea that almost became my last deal as a Clinton administration official. I had been negotiating with the North Koreans since 1997, after it became clear that they were not only testing missiles for their own program but had been shipping missiles and related technology to Iran. The White House responded by slapping sanctions on the North Koreans to get their attention. The next year, as the relationship continued to degrade and missile tests went on unabated, the president asked his former defense secretary, Bill Perry, to make a full review of our relationship with the Kim regime and its nuclear ambitions. Bill brought along his academic partner Ashton Carter, who later became President Obama's secretary of defense, and borrowed me as the inside-government person to join his review team.

Diplomatic relations with the Democratic People's Republic of Korea, or DPRK, as the government is formally known, are a little like the movie *Groundhog Day*—time seems to be caught in a loop as the same events repeat over and over. Then as now, the United States had imposed sanctions to kick-start negotiations after the DPRK launched a missile that flew over Japan. In May 1999, Bill and I traveled to Pyongyang with our small team to meet with senior North Korean officials and deliver a letter from President Clinton offering to back off on sanctions and gradually normalize relations in exchange for major concessions, importantly including ending the North's long-range missile program.

Dealing with North Korea always involves one part normal, if tortuous, diplomacy and one part absurdity. On my first trip to the country with the Perry team, we joined an entourage of North Korean officials on a visit to a rice paddy. Farmers and oxen were working together in a swampy field festooned along one side with signs bearing revolutionary slogans. On the other side of the field was a military band whose members were dressed in pristine white band uniforms, playing revolutionary anthems. It was a surreal scene, one that might have taken place one hundred years ago, in the country's colonial past. One evening on the same trip, Bill and I were treated to a singing performance, in English, of American songs like "My Darling Clementine." For the benefit of the Koreans in attendance, an electronic display scrolled the words to the tunes along the top of the stage, so everyone could sing along. Few did, since most in the audience couldn't read English any better than they could speak it.

You learn to make use of the idiosyncrasies of North Korea's brutal totalitarian behavior. When Bill and I realized that we were not going to get the meeting we'd requested with Kim Jong-Il, the dictator the North Koreans called "Dear Leader," we relied on the certainty that the North Koreans were eavesdropping on all of our conversations to get our point across. While waiting for a meeting to begin, we would discuss what we hoped to convey, knowing we were being listened to. It was an especially useful way to convey messages we might not state quite so directly in a meeting.

It's important to realize that the Kim regime's actions are not the result of irrationality. The bizarre moments, like our visit to the rice paddy, are less the product of a loose screw than of overexuberant socialist propaganda. Similarly, their taunting and illicit missile tests act out a strategy that has proved effective. If the DPRK's behavior under Kim Jong-Il tested the world's patience, it was because he, like his father, and as his son does now, acted according to a paradigm rooted in the idea that the United States is determined to destroy the regime. In his mind, the only way he could guarantee its survival was to have nuclear weapons to deter us from attacking. If you understood his perspective, his behavior was rational.

Indeed, the "Dear Leader" was smart and transactional. He and his top advisers knew precisely what they wanted. At the time I negotiated with them, fourteen extremely technical issues were up for discussion. When Secretary Albright, along with me and our team, made the historic October 2000 trip to Pyongyang, Kim Jong-Il sat with an interpreter and Kang Suk-Ju, my counterpart, and went through each of the points of concern with surprising mastery, answering authoritatively and ignoring only those points on which he didn't hold a strong position.

In a highly technical negotiation, the details are critical. If the leader knows what is being negotiated, it's a good indication that a deal can be made. (Which makes me greatly concerned about how such negotiations will fare under our current president.) I believe that Kim Jong-Il was ready in 2000 to complete a deal over his missile program.

Unfortunately, my country was not ready. As Clinton's time in office wound down, he was pursuing a peace deal in the Middle East and a deal with North Korea with equal vigor. In October 2000, in response to our visit ten months prior, the number-two DPRK official, Vice Marshal Jo Myong-rok, came to Washington with Kang Suk-Ju, the deputy foreign minister and my counterpart. Kang met with me and with Bob Einhorn, our lead missile expert, at the State Department. He had come with a detailed proposal to stop long-range missile testing. If there was any doubt that North Korea was ready to bargain, Vice Marshal Jo invited President Clinton to Pyongyang the following week. When it was made clear to him that one week was clearly not enough time to do that, Jo invited Secretary Albright to come instead—still a nearly impossible request. In the end, Madeleine and I went about two weeks later. Since there was no US embassy in North Korea, we brought in all the staff, supplies, and equipment we needed for an official visit, including a retinue of Marine guards. We even brought a gift, though far from a typical diplomatic one, for the "Dear Leader." Having found out from Kang during his US visit that Kim Jong-Il had every one of Michael Jordan's basketball games on tape, we had arranged to have Jordan sign a basketball, and we presented it to Kim. He was thrilled.

After our initial reception in one of North Korea's dazzlingly ornate meeting rooms, we were told that we'd be going to some sort of special performance. As we set out in a caravan of limousines and vans, I could tell we were heading toward Rungrado Stadium, a sports arena resembling a giant, frosted bundt cake that was built in response to South Korea's hosting the Olympics in 1988. It was a bit disconcerting, since Rungrado was the site of many nationalist events—and several very controversial public executions of Kim Jong-Il's enemies.

Once there, we went up to Kim's viewing box, where we saw that the stadium was filled with thousands of people. In the stands opposite us, the crowd was holding large flip cards, as if they were fans at a college football game. Hundreds of others on the field were performing gymnastics routines in unison. Madeleine and I waited through ten minutes of cheering for the "Dear Leader." As the show progressed, the people in the stands began flipping their signs to produce animated murals of scenes portraying the DPRK's greatness and missiles whizzing. They were clearly intended to impress us with the country's military prowess, but what they really brought home was how attached to its missiles the government was, and how much was at stake for the regime in giving them up in the name of an understanding with the United States. As the show went on, Madeleine and I tried to smile as if we were enjoying the display. If we looked unhappy, we thought, we might insult Kim and squelch the possible deal. As a mock flip-card Taepodong missile was launched, Kim turned first to the secretary and then to me, saying, through his interpreter, that perhaps this would be the last launch of such a missile. The message was unmistakable. We smiled on.

Our frozen smiles played worse at home than in Pyongyang. When footage of our visit to Rungrado Stadium was aired back in the United States, Madeleine was criticized for looking too approving. It should have been an indication of the disappointment that was to come.

The negotiations continued, and we looked to be very close to a deal. The American media, sensing the breakthrough, kept a constant watch on whether I would return to North Korea, pestering me so often that at a good-bye reception at the State Department for diplomatic press as the Clinton administration wound down, I sported a sign, tied with ribbon from my neck, reading NO DECISION YET to fend off the repeated inquiries.

Nonetheless, when Madeleine traveled to Africa for her last overseas trip as secretary in December, I lugged woolen garb and a winter coat through equatorial countries with 100-degree days, not knowing if the president would dispatch me to North Korea to seal the details or arrange what would have been a historic visit by President Clinton to sign a deal.

I never went to Pyongyang again. Between the president's Middle East negotiations and the uncertainty over the outcome of the presidential election, we simply ran out of time.

As we know, George W. Bush was declared the winner of the highly contested 2000 election. After that strange month we all spent discussing hanging chads and vote recounts, I drove out with my key team members to the Virginia home of Colin Powell. We gathered in the dining room with General Powell, now President Bush's incoming secretary of state, and Condoleezza Rice, the incoming national security adviser, to brief them on what we'd advanced in Pyongyang. Powell was receptive, telling me that the Bush White House would be wise to "play this hand." Rice was less so. President-Elect Bush, she said, would want to do a policy review before deciding how to proceed.

As I went about moving out of my office at State and settling into a new job, I waited to see what would happen. A couple of months later, in March, as South Korean president Kim Dae-Jung was arriving in Washington for a meeting with President Bush, Powell told reporters that he would be following the Clinton administration's lead on negotiating with North Korea—only to announce the next day that President Kim's "sunshine policy" was no longer the US objective. Dispatched by the president from a meeting with the South Koreans to inform the press of the new direction, Powell said that he had gotten "too far forward" on his skis. Our initiative was dead.

In addition to the disappointment of the election, I had to process the disheartening realization that my team and I might have wrestled a viable deal out of a tyrannical regime, only to have it negated by a Supreme Court ruling on a ballot recount in Florida.

The key to surviving tough times like these is to step back and look at the larger picture. Is there some good that's going to come from what seems like wasted effort? Is it time to dig deeper or walk away? Taking stock of what you may have gained, despite seeming failure, might allow you to offer someone else support, or nurse yourself through. At times it's all you can do, and I've done my best, even as I've watched North Korea become the world's foremost nuclear threat.

I recall that at a dark moment in the Iran negotiation, when failure seemed certain, John Kerry said, "Sometimes you have to meet and not get anywhere in order to one day get somewhere."

This has been true repeatedly in my career, and it's a lesson that working women especially must learn. One of my greatest moments of professional pride was when I became the first woman undersecretary for political affairs. But perhaps my biggest moment of disappointment came from wanting to be the first woman deputy secretary of state.

In the spring of 2014, Bill Burns, the deputy secretary and my predecessor as "P," announced that he planned to retire from the Foreign Service in the fall, after an extraordinary career of more than thirty years. The buzz began immediately about possible candidates to follow in his footsteps. I wanted to be respectful of the president's and Secretary Kerry's selection process while at the same time ensuring I was given real consideration. I carefully let Kerry's chief of staff know of my interest. I heard that others, particularly other senior women in the department, were urging the secretary to recommend me to the president. Finally, after many weeks of uncertainty, Secretary Kerry and I had a conversation, and he told me he was recommending me.

News of his decision spread throughout the department, as these things inevitably do, and many employees gave me their congratulations. I always replied that I appreciated their support but reminded them that nothing was final. As we neared the end of Bill's time without a decision announced, National Security Adviser Susan Rice suggested that some influential men in the White House were supporting Tony Blinken, a colleague with whom I'd worked well since the Clinton years, a longtime aide to Vice President Biden, and now Susan's very competent deputy and someone who had been with President Obama since the beginning. When I objected that Kerry's chief of staff had assured me that the president had said it was Kerry's decision, it was Susan's turn to remind me that, in Washington, no job is certain until you are sitting in the chair.

On a Friday, the eve of Yom Kippur, the holiest day in the Jewish calendar, Secretary Kerry called me to his office. The president, he informed me, had decided on Tony. I hardly had time to absorb the news when I got a message that Susan wanted to see me. When I went to her office, Susan expressed her personal sympathies, but said she had a good idea for me: to take the open US Agency for International Development job. USAID is an important post overseeing the nation's disaster and development funds overseas, but it was clearly a consolation prize. As Susan spoke, I could not stop the tears—part out of anger, part out of sorrow.

Back at State, I packed up to go home to a final meal before the Yom Kippur fast and evening services at our synagogue. I spent the holiday—the Jewish rites of repentance and forgiveness—in mourning, reflecting on all that had occurred and finding some peace inside myself.

When I got back to work on Monday, I asked Secretary Kerry if he would recommend to the president naming me acting deputy until Tony was confirmed by the Senate. The president and secretary agreed (meaning that, officially, I was the first female to sit in the chair, even if I wasn't to be permanently appointed). I also let Susan know that I did not think the USAID position made sense in the short time left in the administration. I urged them to hire someone who knew the agency well. (I often remind myself and others that, after the honor, there is the work, and you must want to do the work.)

Part of letting go of the disappointment of not becoming deputy secretary of state was accepting what I got instead: had I replaced Bill as deputy then, I probably would not have continued to lead the work on the Iran deal, one of the singular accomplishments of my time at State, and a signature achievement of the Obama era.

I don't mean to say that letting go always means taking it on the chin. The tendency to try to control one's life too closely can inhibit us from saying yes to opportunities that might change our lives. In January 1994, I was at home one Sunday night having dinner with friends when the phone rang. On the other end was Tom Donilon, an old friend whom I'd gotten to know in 1984, when he was a delegate counter for Walter Mondale's presidential campaign against Ronald Reagan. Most recently, I'd heard that Tom had been hired to be chief of staff for Warren Christopher, the incoming secretary of state nominated by the young new Democratic president from Arkansas, Bill Clinton. "Christopher wants to see you," Tom said. "Can you come in tomorrow to talk?"

The next day was Martin Luther King Day, a holiday, and just days before Clinton's inauguration. The streets of Washington were practically deserted as I drove to the transition offices at the State Department where Christopher, still waiting to be confirmed, had set up shop.

I had only the vaguest sense of why Christopher would want to see me. I knew that he was putting together his staff while he waited to be approved by the Senate. But what I knew was campaigning, congressional work, and community organizing. When it came to foreign affairs, I had only the basic expertise I'd picked up from campaigning, working in Congress, and sharing shop talk with my journalist husband, who at that time wrote about international trade and economics for the *National Journal*, the insider's magazine in Washington.

What's more, I had a job. Two years before, David Doak and Bob Shrum, political consultants who between them had had a hand in every major Democratic campaign of my adulthood, from George McGovern to Ted Kennedy (and Barbara Mikulski), had asked me to become a partner in their political media firm. My name was on the door. It was, for me, an uncharacteristically predictable step, but a remunerative one. I knew what I was doing. I was happy.

Dapper, deliberate in his manner, and a reserved presence in front of the television cameras, Christopher in person had a sparkle in his eye that immediately put me at ease. "You've been recommended to me. Pending the president-elect's approval, I'd like you to consider being the assistant secretary for legislative affairs."

Other than what the title implied—representing the State Department to Congress—I had no idea what the job was. "If you want someone who knows everything there is to know about foreign policy, then I am not the person," I told Christopher. Then, sensing that this wasn't why he was interested in me, I went on. "If you are looking for someone who knows how Washington works, who's been on the Hill, then maybe I'm the right person."

Christopher, of course, had a good idea how Washington worked. He had been deputy secretary of state under President Carter and was experienced in the ways of the capital. But he'd been back in California since Carter left office more than a decade before, and he had never enjoyed dealing with Capitol Hill. He wanted someone who could wrangle Congress and keep them at bay.

I left Christopher, telling him I'd think about it. The next day I went to my partners at Doak, Shrum, Harris and Sherman. David and Bob both thought I should take the job. "Who knows?" said Bob. "You might be the first woman secretary of state."

I could have answered that I didn't want to be secretary of state, that I didn't want to throw my life in the air to pursue a course I'd never imagined for myself—that I didn't want to give up my sense that I was the one calling the shots in my life. But after some deliberation, and discussion with my husband, I picked up the phone and told Tom Donilon that if the president-elect and Christopher wanted to nominate me, I'd be honored. I've never turned back. The world became my caseload.

Letting go can represent a leap forward, no less in our personal lives than in our work. When I was twenty, I got married. Alfred Singer and I had known each other since we were children. We seemed perfectly matched. His father was in real estate like mine, and we had more than once been hauled to Ocean City, Maryland, with our families during the Maryland Real Estate Association convention. In fact, on our first date we went to a movie in Ocean City. He was my date for my senior prom. When I showed up for my freshman year at Smith College in Northampton, Massachusetts, he was starting his junior year at Trinity College in Hartford, Connecticut, just forty miles south.

Alfred wasn't my first love, or first boyfriend. I had dated other guys, but only one other hit my heart deeply—Michael, from Winchester,

Virginia, whom I'd met at a weekend retreat for Jewish youth when I was still in high school. By the time I got to Smith, however, I was committed to Alfred. We soon got caught up in a group of Smith-Trinity couples. Every Thursday evening, we women trekked down to Hartford, since guys staying at Smith was out of the question. When Michael called from Yale, which he now attended, I told him I couldn't see him. Now I wonder if that was a mistake, but there was no turning back. Not long after, one couple in our group, rising seniors, announced their engagement. Before I knew it, Alfred and I were pinned—I would now wear Alfred's fraternity pin, one step short of an engagement.

I struggle sometimes to explain to young people how I could have given up a Smith education for early marriage. For one thing, even at a school where women were the leaders, the expectation of marriage upon graduation was still a norm, confirmed by a ritual in which all the senior women, dressed in caps and gowns, would roll hoops down the quad in a race to see who would marry first! It wasn't unusual for women to leave college to marry and not look back. For the ambitious among us, like me, getting married proved that we could have it all, and do it all.

And I did love Alfred, as much as a twenty-year-old can, and with that, naturally, came other considerations. The sexual revolution was under way, but just. Premarital sex was acceptable, but mostly if you had already planned to get married eventually.

Strange as it sounds, I think marriage, for both of us, was our chosen method of rebelling against our parents. It was a way to separate from my powerful family, to chart my own course. The fact that I had to separate by attaching to someone else shows that I was not ready. I was just beginning to understand my own power but was still too afraid to own it myself.

Alfred's mother and father were very much against the marriage, but not because they were worried about us owning our power. They thought I had lured Alfred into proposing in order to get a ring on my finger, when in fact I was the one who had suggested that we put it off until he got back from the Peace Corps, which he planned to do after college. It took a stern conversation with our rabbi about the potential loss of their son to finally convince Alfred's parents to attend the wedding.

My parents were outwardly supportive, though in later years my sister told me that she and my father had cried at the wedding, not out of joy but concern.

We married in the chapel of our synagogue in June 1969. I wore a short white-lace dress and a veil. The reception, held at the very formal Ambassador Hotel in Baltimore, was a sit-down luncheon that seems staid and scripted to me now. For our four days of honeymoon in Montreal, I had bought a pale blue going-away outfit, hat included, and a black cocktail dress with cutouts on the sides; I felt very sophisticated and grown-up. Almost immediately afterward, we moved to Boston, where Alfred was starting law school at Boston College in the fall. That first summer, Alfred drove a cab and I worked for the Maryknoll Fathers, registering contributions and doing other clerical tasks.

When fall came, I didn't entirely mind that I wasn't going back to Smith. Opposition to the Vietnam War was spurring protests on college campuses and on the streets—everywhere, it seemed, but sleepy Northampton. Now enrolled at Boston University, I was no longer cut off from the action. I could attend classes, work part-time—and march.

Alfred and I made our home in a small apartment on Ransom Road in the Brighton neighborhood—a bedroom, a small living room, and a kitchen that accommodated a small table that could seat four. The bathroom was so small that a chunk of the door was cut out to get past the toilet. I acted out the life of a model wife. I sewed curtains and pillows and tried to re-create the recipes from the *New York Times Sunday Magazine,* or else I'd spin the Minute Rice wheel to see which meat to combine with which soup and rice and bake up in a casserole. I even had white note cards with MRS. ALFRED LEE SINGER on them. Our parents provided enough financial support to get us through when combined with my earnings. We considered ourselves very lucky, privileged, and blessed.

And we were. I liked organizing teenagers in a Boston housing project and working with teenagers at a Jewish community center. Alfred's law school colleagues became our social group, and together we charted our way through three years of law school. Once I graduated from BU, I worked as a social worker at the Middlesex County Hospital for the chronically and terminally ill.

Alfred's parents wanted him to join a Baltimore law firm and made introductions. But in a letter to the managing partner, Alfred said, no doubt encouraged by me, that he was interested only if the firm had a robust pro bono practice. His parents were mortified. Alfred began to look for other opportunities. Georgia Legal Services fit the bill, and after Alfred took the state bar, we settled in Savannah, where Alfred worked for legal aid. We agreed that after two years we'd swap career priorities, and I would go to graduate school in social work, back north.

It was during this time that I began to have doubts about our marriage, though I could not articulate them clearly to myself or to Alfred. No doubt, my consciousness-raising group made me more reflective. I began to question what a marriage should be like and what our relationship needed to be to survive. I began to feel that Alfred was living my life, not his, and that emotionally we were entirely different. When we disagreed, I wanted to talk things out; he believed in the silent treatment. I was an organizer and activist; at heart, he was not. I felt that my world was becoming larger while his seemed to be shrinking. We soldiered on, but I wondered more and more about our future together.

In 1974, we moved to Washington, DC, where Alfred went to work for Ralph Nader's Public Citizen and I commuted to social work school at the University of Maryland at Baltimore. I did extremely well in school and outside class became a student leader and avid community organizer. I was finding my voice, flush with my success and evident ability to organize. Like Gloria Steinem, our icon in the '70s, I kept my hair long and wore blue jeans and turtlenecks. A friend who noticed me biting my nails one day told me she was relieved to see that I was not perfect.

In fact, I was far from perfect. My marriage was feeling crumbly and tentative. Alfred was clearly unhappy, and I felt that one reason was that he was living my values more than his own—he really wasn't interested in bucking authority. He preferred Buicks, well-made suits, and a more ordered life. Now, with a cohort of friends who saw themselves the way I did, the distance between us grew. We began counseling, both together and me alone. The central issue for me was whether I had a right to my own space, separate and apart from my husband. Clearly, I was becoming me, on my own.

Ultimately, I decided that I needed to complete the separation I had begun from my own family, which really meant separating from and subsequently divorcing Alfred. Initially I moved in with a classmate, but finally, on my twenty-sixth birthday, I moved into an efficiency apartment in Baltimore and, for the first time, lived alone, except for the cockroaches.

Nowadays, looking back, my marriage to Alfred seems like some-one else's life. I knew I was not what he needed and vice versa. It helps, of course, to have been lucky to find love again in my marriage to Bruce, and to have our daughter, Sarah, and now our two toddler grandsons.

I sometimes talk about my first marriage as a false start that ended in a brick wall, but it's closer to the truth to say that it was a necessary bridge to who I am today, a period of testing the bonds that held me back. I knew then that I had to let go of Alfred to gain myself, and I hoped that Alfred would find the same freedom to be who he was.

I can't end a chapter about accepting loss and letting go without addressing the painful highs and lows of politics. Anyone whose life is ruled in part by elections, as mine has been, knows that winning and losing are not always what they seem. Even as long as I've been connected to electoral politics, it doesn't get any easier—in fact, as my opportunity to serve comes to a close, it might get harder. The last election was one of the most painful of my life.

A decade ago, I spent the evening of my birthday, June 7, watch-ing television with tears pouring down my cheeks as Hillary Clinton addressed a packed ballroom in Washington, accepting defeat in her quest for the Democratic nomination for president. For so many of us who had come of political age at the confluence of the women's movement and the civil rights movement, it was a wrenching mo-ment. Democrats were about to nominate the first African American presidential candidate, but it came at the expense of the first woman.

Eight years later, I got the birthday party I wanted. On June 7, 2016, Hillary was poised to claim the Democratic nomination with a speech in a Brooklyn warehouse, and I had asked my sister and my daughter to join me. It was a fantastic evening, ending with a meaningful handshake of thanks from Hillary for the work I had done for the campaign. The evening energized all of us to do more, including Sarah, who had voted for Bernie Sanders in the primary but now felt the importance of this historical moment and became an ardent Hillary supporter.

Like so many others, I redoubled the efforts I'd been making during the primary. I became part of a transition team that began writing papers and thinking through what those first two hundred days would look like. I couldn't help but feel flattered by the newspaper articles that added my name to the list of possible nominees for secretary of state, deputy secretary, or UN ambassador. I also knew that, in the ways of Washington, these outcomes were unlikely—what thrilled me about a Hillary presidency was what it would mean for the country to have a woman president, and what she could get done, given her depth of knowledge and experience.

A few days out from the election, I flew overnight to London for twenty-four hours to do two successful fundraising events with campaign chair John Podesta. With election night upon us, I couldn't stay put. If history was to be made, I wanted to be in the room if I could. I made plans, with Bruce, to go to New York and spend the evening at the Javits Center, where Hillary's campaign would rally on election night. The enormous room was packed, already jubilant.

As the Florida results started to come in, things were definitely amiss, but I took heart from a chat with Donna Shalala, the former Clinton cabinet member and a longtime president of the University of Miami. The early returns, Donna felt confident, would turn in Hillary's favor as the votes from Miami came in. When she swung by my spot on the floor again, we both knew that the election was literally heading south and away from Hillary. By 9:00 p.m., elation was turning to misery. It began to sink in not only that Hillary had lost, but that Donald Trump would be our president.

Bruce and I stayed up to watch the dismal commentary and final results on TV from our hotel room, trying to absorb what had happened. Sometime after Bruce took an early train back to DC to get to a meeting, I forced myself to head over to Penn Station alone. I was waiting for my train, nibbling a bagel-and-egg sandwich and sipping coffee in one of the fast-food alcoves at the station, when my daughter called my cell phone. I had held it together until then. I broke into tears and sorrow, very deep sorrow.

There have been many days since when I have wanted to pack up and lean out. In the new age calculus, age seventy, we're told, is the new sixty. But now that I'm sixty-nine, the chances that I will get to serve my country again in government are slim. I see that people and our planet are being hurt. People who lost jobs because of trade or technology still feel alone and lost in an age of rapid social and technological change. Women see their reproductive rights challenged again and their health care choices evaporating. Refugees and immigrants who are so much a part of our greatness live in fear of deportation and discrimination. Many citizens don't feel safe and secure, neither physically nor economically.

Like so many others, I have days when I'm depressed, days when I think our country is headed in the wrong direction, days when family problems bring sorrow. But during these moments when it feels hopeless, I go back to what I know: we must learn from our experiences and use that knowledge as inspiration as we get up and try again.

Indeed, the day after President Trump's inauguration, millions of women marched in streets all over the country and all over the world.

My daughter and her friends came to Washington to take up the banner that we older women had flown for so long. As they were making signs in our kitchen the night before, I commented, "I can't believe I'm still protesting this BS." They insisted that comment become my sign, one that was recognized with grateful nods the next day as women, and men, joined in hopeful solidarity. That march produced scores of women who have since been moved to run for office. In the year that followed, more than twenty thousand prospective female candidates had contacted EMILY's List, asking how to mount a run. With a year to go until the 2018 midterms, more than four hundred women had taken serious steps toward running for Congress, from both parties. Nearly forty of them are running for the Senate, ten times the number of women who ran in the previous two cycles, according to the *New York Times*. Whether they succeed or not—and it's inevitable that many will fail in their first try—it's exhilarating to know that even after what we've been through, so many want to give it a try.

The digital world, once alien to my generation, has become an organizing tool so powerful that grassroots organizers like the group Indivisible can reach out to people everywhere to create change. When President Trump pulled out of the Paris climate agreement, mayors and governors committed to pressing on with the agreement's objectives and targets. People have taken failure and turned it into personal and political power.

Recently, at an airport, I spotted a gaggle of preteen girls sporting the same gray T-shirt. The shirts said, SHE BELIEVED SHE COULD SO SHE DID. I asked the adult team leader what the group was. It turned out they were Girl Scouts headed to a celebration in New Orleans. Having been a Girl Scout myself, I was thrilled that the Scouts had become a place of empowerment and service.

As soon as I got to work the day after Hillary's loss, I sat down to write a letter to everyone at the firm where I worked, the Albright Stonebridge Group. It was a bit of therapy for myself, even as I hoped it would touch others. I recalled the late 1960s and '70s and my own political coming of age. It had been an extraordinarily violent time. Assassination of the president and his brother, assassination of three civil rights leaders, violence on college campuses, riots in city streets, death to those registering voters. But that time eventually led to the codification of civil rights into law, advances in the cause of women, and an end to the Vietnam War.

Change now, like then, will not come quickly. We live in such a divided nation and strain to listen to each other, cocooned in our favorite TV shows and podcasts, shutting out the possibility of any common narrative. But abetting the failure of our democracy is not an option. We may not succeed at first, but there is no choice but to mourn our loss and then to try and try again.

chapter five

BUILDING YOUR TEAM

As we made the push toward the final Iran agreement, the fifteen Americans on my core negotiating team sat around our delegation room at the Palais Coburg in Vienna casting the movie we seemed to be stuck in. We called it *The Coburg Affair*. Ted Danson was the obvious choice to play Secretary Kerry. The Spanish actor Javier Bardem's coif in *No Country for Old Men* made him a dead ringer for Secretary of Energy Ernest Moniz. Kevin Kline—with a mustache—would play Deputy Secretary of State Bill Burns. *Home Alone*'s Macaulay Culkin was unquestionably the perfect Jake Sullivan, Burns's eternally youthful partner in the back-channel negotiations. I was told that my part would be played by Meryl Streep in *Devil Wears Prada* mode, though I was assured that the likeness was due entirely to the similarities in our hairstyles, not to any resemblance between me and the dragon lady Streep portrayed in the movie. Our movie felt like one of those classic caper flicks that brings together a bunch of motley safe-crackers, getaway drivers, dynamiters, and other specialists. Instead, we were a cast of nuclear experts, lawyers, and career diplomats.

Vienna may bring out the Hollywood in us Americans. It's a natural movie-set backdrop, as you know if you've ever seen *The Third Man*, Orson Welles's moody, conspiratorial evocation of postwar Vienna. It's still a town so full of spies and diplomatic intrigue that we all just assumed that we were being overheard or electronically surveilled. My British counterpart and I discussed the number of centrifuges the deal would allow Iran to operate by passing slips of paper back and forth on the outdoor patio of my room.

Despite the glamourous setting, ours would have been a snoozer of a movie. It would have included far too many scenes of us huddled in hotel rooms, flipping through briefing books and calculating the intersecting variables of uranium enrichment levels, spent nuclear fuel rods, and centrifuge specifications.

And eating. One day in Vienna, our press liaison, Marie Harf (to be played by Kirsten Dunst), was looking for a color story to keep the expectant reporters happy and asked us to catalog our snacking habits. We reckoned that the fifteen of us on the American core negotiating team had worked our way through ten pounds of Twizzlers, thirty pounds of mixed nuts and dried fruit, twenty pounds of string cheese, and more than two hundred Rice Krispies treats, all in less than a month. The Coburg was solicitous of our stomachs as well. Conscious that our twenty-seven-day run would unexpectedly go through the Fourth of July, the manager set up an American-style barbecue on an outdoor patio, complete with hot dogs, hamburgers, and corn on the cob.

We had help from home too. After I wrote an email thanking all the spouses, partners, and families of the core team for their understanding over the weeks of being deprived of their loved ones, one family shipped over sock puppets to comfort and entertain us and homemade baked goods.

Over four years and thousands of miles of travel, we had grown into a team, with inside jokes, nicknames, and a recognition that each of us had a talent and a temperament essential to getting us to the finish line.

We saw ourselves as a trusty, overworked squad sent by our government to get an impossible mission done, but we were just in the front-facing position of a huge force that extended behind us deep into the government. Hundreds of government personnel were brought into this extraordinary effort by dint of their department jobs. Adam Szubin, the Treasury Department sanctions expert who traveled with us for the first two years, followed by Felicia Swindells, had behind them the Office of Foreign Assets Control, along with the State Department's Richard Nephew and later Christopher Backemeyer. Lead State lawyer Newell Highsmith and his deputy Kimberly Gahan were essential. Our efforts were backed up by analysts at the CIA, the National Security Agency (NSA), the United States Mission to the United Nations (USUN), and the Pentagon. As we came down to the wire, staffers at the US nuclear labs in New Mexico, Illinois, and Tennessee made their top-tier teams available 24/7 to answer technical questions from us, in real time. We employed lawyers, embassy personnel, congressional liaisons, typists, and assistants who often shared the same crazy hours and disruptions to their family lives, with nowhere near the recognition for their efforts that the president, Secretary Kerry, Secretary Moniz, or even I got for ours.

That just accounts for the Americans. The P5+1 nations and the EU had their own teams and their own phalanxes of foreign affairs, financial, legal, and scientific experts and staff. There were teams within teams within teams.

◇◇◇◇◇◇◇◇◇◇

Having all these resources was awe-inspiring, but it also required forging a consensus out of many competing streams of data, expertise, and opinion. My chief task as lead negotiator for the most prominent nation on our side of the table was to keep all the various teams headed in the same direction. Building consensus is an extremely time-intensive exercise, one that requires a series of mini-negotiations with interested parties to elicit their cooperation, taking the best of what they have to offer without getting bogged down in their particular needs.

In the Iran nuclear deal, this process took hours of discussion with all of my partners—I negotiated within the administration, with members of both parties in Congress, with each member nation of the EU and the P5+1, with Israel and the Gulf States, with South Korea, Japan, India, Italy, and Australia, and with other allies and partners who were not at the table. I sought advice and support from NGOs, think tanks, and advocacy groups that look out for populations and policy in the Middle East. (Occasionally, I like to joke, I actually negotiated with Iran.) The care and feeding of each individual player serves you when you have to call on them at crunch-time.

For me, the absolute center of all these concentric circles was the "deputies" meeting held in the White House Situation Room, so named because these meetings convened the number-two officials in the relevant departments of the US government and their closest colleagues: the deputy national security adviser, Tom Donilon (and later Denis McDonough and Tony Blinken); the vice chairman of the Joint Chiefs of Staff, Admiral Sandy Winnefeld; Michele Flournoy, undersecretary of defense for policy at the Department of Defense (later replaced by Jim Miller and Christine Wormuth); and David Cohen, who, as undersecretary, ran the Treasury Department's antiterrorist finance unit and later became deputy CIA director. The USUN sent a representative, as did the Energy Department, the intelligence services, and any other federal agency that might help us set the table for the next round of the negotiation. Each person at the meeting would give a preview of what the Iranians might ask for, identify positions we had to protect, and generally air their concerns. We'd also spend some time on "tabletop exercises"—not literally pushing model ships around a table map, as the term implies, but gaming out the scenarios that might come up at the talks and how to respond. These meetings began almost as soon as I joined the negotiations in the fall of 2011 and continued to be convened until the deal was finished. If need be, any deputy could join in by secure video conference from wherever they were in the world.

The decisions we made in those meetings filtered back through the deputies to guide the massively coordinated effort that spanned the Hill to the White House, to Foggy Bottom, and across the Potomac to the Pentagon, then around the world. We repositioned our military in the Persian Gulf and commissioned and deployed a new bomb that could penetrate the once-secret underground enrichment facility called Fordow, backing up our diplomacy with credible threats of force. We increased sanctions, and Treasury and State sent out tandem teams to enforce them. Since many countries had to reduce their imports of Iranian oil under sanctions, the Energy and State Departments worked together to urge other oil-exporting countries to increase production, and we helped match them with new oil supply contracts so we didn't tank the world economy in the process of wrestling with Iran. We kept the lines open to Congress, not least the Republicans, who were lining up to oppose the deal before it was even finished. I put out an offer of a one-on-one briefing to every member of Congress. I was surprised when one of the most virulently opposed senators, Tom Cotton of Arkansas, took me up on it. He was in DC during an August congressional recess waiting for the birth of his first child and so came by my office at State. For more than an hour, we had as long and probing a conversation as I've had with anyone from his side of the aisle on the deal. I didn't expect to, and I didn't convince him.

Consensus had to flow up the organization chart as well, of course. If some new tack might change government policy and therefore require a decision from our bosses, first Tom Donilon and then Susan Rice, as national security adviser, would call meetings with the principals—cabinet members, the Joint Chiefs chair, and other top dogs. Before a gathering of the principals, we'd prepare a briefing book that gave Secretary Kerry a deep dive into the topics being covered, and often we'd pay a visit to the principals of other government sectors to brief them and sow the seeds of consensus going into the meeting. If we had to get sign-off from the top, the National Security Council would be formally convened, triggering the attendance of the president and the vice president. At these tightly run meetings, President Obama would listen, ask questions, and then clearly give guidance about how he wanted to proceed. Having clear marching orders from the top is critical to maintaining consensus.

<><><><><><><><>

The weeks before a new round of talks with the Iranians were spent getting everyone on the P5+1 side on the same footing. There was a constant chatter among the diplomats at my level, both in person and via secure phone calls and emails. I'd check in constantly with the Israelis, who, as the primary target of Iran's aggressive rhetoric, had, as they say, an existential interest in the progress of the talks. They also had some of the best technical experts, and we made use of their professionals for validation and critique of various ideas. I made occasional use of a dedicated secure phone line we had at the State Department to the desk of Sergey Ryabkov, my Russian counterpart. The buzz got louder, and the chat sessions got more formal, as we neared a meeting with the Iranians.

The endless meetings and conference calls usually began with a secure video conference or phone call with our European colleagues, and the Russians and Chinese commonly consulted beforehand as well. That would be followed by a conference call with all of our P5+1 colleagues, led by Helga. Cathy Ashton would call an in-person coordinating meeting a week or two before each round as well, to ensure that we had a game plan and consensus. Each of us held bilateral consultations, often traveling to each other's capitals for talks. The ambassadors from the Gulf Cooperation Council states—Bahrain, Kuwait, Oman, Qatar, Saudi Arabia, and the United Arab Emirates—would convene with me and my staff in a conference room on the seventh floor of State for a briefing before each round (and a debrief afterward). All of these meetings spawned pre-meetings and the preparation of briefing books and more phone calls and emails.

Sometimes, especially as we got to the endgame and the sessions with the Iranians came closer together, the preparation for one session would begin before we'd completely wrapped up the previous one. By the time of our final round at the Coburg, much of our preparation for the meeting happened on the ground in Vienna.

When we got to what became the final round, each day began with a series of bilateral meetings with each team, then an overall P5+1 coordination before we went into negotiations with the Iranians. Often there were awkward blocks of time as we consulted with each other and the Iranians cooled their heels, waiting for us to get an internal consensus. During these lag times, our team and others were usually doing intricate mathematical calculations to ensure that changing one element wouldn't undermine the overall objective, working with lawyers to ensure that the language would really get the desired result, consulting with economists and lawyers to understand the impact of any lifting of sanctions, and talking with the International Atomic Energy Agency and our own experts to button down the verification and monitoring mechanisms and regime.

It was a staggeringly laborious process, especially considering that at the same time I was doing my everyday job as "P" at State, coordinating and advising personnel all over the world. I once joined a National Security Council meeting with President Obama from Zambia at one in the morning local time.

◇◇◇◇◇◇◇◇◇◇

The model I always think of when trying to build consensus is "the Perry process," which I observed up close after Bill Perry asked Madeleine Albright if he could borrow me for his North Korea policy review in 1997. As mentioned earlier, Bill had assembled a team of nuclear experts and negotiators that included his colleague Ashton Carter as well as the nuclear experts Bob Einhorn and Jim Timbie, both of whom would work on the Iran deal with me. Our orders were to seek out everyone who knew anything about North Korea—every scientist, every agency official, and every think tank from Washington to South Korea, Japan, and China, to Russia and North Korea itself. Over ten months, we gathered every point of view available. By the time we were done, we knew all the sensitivities of the region, what had been tried, and what was possible, and we were able to combine what we'd learned into a well-informed, well-formulated policy that the president embraced. It ended in a potential deal, as discussed in the last chapter, that came within a hanging chad of stopping North Korea from testing long-range missiles.

The Perry process was predicated on shared information. As I worked to bring my Iran team to consensus, I stressed that we were all interlocking pieces of a single team and we all had to know every part of the deal. Once the real negotiating had begun in the summer of 2013, after Hassan Rouhani had been elected president of Iran, I asked our interagency players who would form the core negotiating team to draft a complete version of the entire agreement as we saw it, setting down on paper the basic agreement along with all of the technical annexes—more than one hundred pages. We all knew that what we wrote would not be final, but I wanted my team to know the larger goal, no matter what portion of the deal they were working on.

For two days, we sat as a team in the secure deputy's conference room along Mahogany Row—the ornately decorated area on State's seventh floor where the secretary and his or her three top officers sit—and went through the document line by line so we all understood what we were heading for. Those of us who weren't nuclear physicists would have the technical language explained to us, and the scientists would learn the sensitivities of the politics. If some of us had trouble making sense of a section of the agreement, we changed the language so that it was clear even to the unschooled. We didn't want any obscure technical talk in the final agreement. It was important that all of us who were negotiating it understood it, and that we could explain it to those we were negotiating for.

The other advantage of walking everyone through the deal was that each member of the team learned the limits of their technical knowledge and who on the team knew what they did not. While I wanted everyone to be acquainted with what the agreement contained, I didn't expect any member to negotiate out of their depth. Our intensives on the seventh floor ensured that we all could attach a face and a name to every section of the agreement, from nukes to sanctions.

Preparing in this rigorous way helped us develop a road map, even if a lot of detours and rerouting lay ahead. Preparation gave us power in the negotiating room, since each of us would have formed our own ideas about each section and the deal as a whole. Each one of us would also have sufficient technical expertise to know what was at stake for all the others and the language to talk about it.

Not least, seeing all the competing elements that we needed to solve laid out in one place, we all came to understand just how difficult it was going to be to get an agreement.

◇◇◇◇◇◇◇◇◇◇

Another reason sharing the whole agreement with everyone was important was that it established not only what we were working toward but how we would work. Anyone who has ever worked for me knows that I have a set of norms that move with me from job to job. Norms are great levelers for any group working toward a common goal. No matter the pay grade, title, or relative wealth of experience of the members of the team, norms apply to everyone.

The first norm is that everyone should be at the same table every day. When we worked as a team in the actual negotiation, we met as a group early in the morning, and then again late at night, everyone at the same table, no matter what their job. Unless some information was particularly sensitive or required a special security clearance, everyone heard the same brief. The unmistakable message of this norm is that everyone is trusted to be part of the team. Everyone is invited (and expected) to contribute. By extension, we move as a group; individuals don't go their own way.

What this also means is that if you're on my team, I trust that you'll bring your skepticism, your questions, and your doubts to the table as well. I don't want to hear about your thoughts from someone else, or from outside the group. That takes a bit of trust on the team members' part as well, faith that I'll listen and take action if needed. My experience is that every group has its skeptics, people who aren't satisfied with the consensus. I find it critical that they speak up, no matter where in the process they choose to do so. In the last days of the Iran negotiation, I was finishing up a report back to Washington when Jim Timbie came in to see me. He quietly suggested that I meet with Paul, a young colleague who was smart and creative and decidedly one of the skeptics on the team.

It took a lot of patience for me to stop the momentum toward the finish line at that moment to hear what we'd left out. But Timbie impressed on me that Paul's concerns had to be addressed. Paul, a young analyst and nonproliferation expert, presented me with a list of fifty-two items. I took a deep breath, told him where we could sit down, and said, "Well, okay, walk me through them." I listened, and then told him to take them to Ernie Moniz, as most of them involved technical details. By the time the deal was done, virtually all of those fifty-two items were in the deal. It wasn't easy, but in the end we had buy-in from every member of the team, and that was incredibly valuable.

Cathy Ashton also made efforts to solidify the disparate casts of the P5+1 countries into a cohesive team, as did her successor, Federica Mogherini. During the frustrating summer of 2014, the nearly one hundred of us on all seven teams spent several days in Vienna holding seminars, suggested by Cathy, on the various topics covered in any expected agreement, with each country presenting on an assigned topic. The German team led us all, including Iran, through a discussion on nuclear transparency. The Chinese spoke to the group about Iran's Arak reactor and what it would take to bring it up to international standards. We Americans held forth on centrifuge technology. The whole exercise had the air of a high school science fair, but it drove home that we would have to operate in unison, shouldering different specialties and letting no one or two teams do all the heavy lifting.

It's crucial during a time of consensus-building to allow as many ideas as possible to be offered and considered. Ideas are the life-blood of any resolution process, and it's in everyone's best interest to let them flow, even if many of them won't survive to the end. Even the strangest ideas may evolve into something workable, or spur thought in another mind and lead to a workable plan. Other ideas are placeholders—they capture the parameters of a particular problem without resolving them satisfactorily.

Early in the P5+1 talks, we were tussling with the problem of replacing Iran's nuclear reactor being built at Arak, which, when completed, would provide Iran with a steady source of fissionable plutonium in its spent fuel rods. Everyone knew we needed to shut down Arak, but how would we furnish Iran with a new-generation reactor, one that could produce electricity without producing bomb makings at the same time? And how would we do it promptly enough to satisfy Iran that we weren't simply taking down their alternative-energy plans?

Cathy suggested, for instance, that we build a modern reactor beside the existing one at Arak and when it was finished, destroy the old one. Unfortunately, technical experts determined that it would take far too long to construct a new reactor and Iran would be able to gather spent fuel rods long past the beginning of the deal. Although we didn't think the two-reactors concept should go into a final deal, at that moment it was good enough to get us past the problem so that we could move on to more basic questions—how many centrifuges, what types, how large a stockpile of enriched uranium, how enriched, and so forth. The Ashton plan stayed in the drafts of the deal for a long time before it was finally dismissed toward the end of the negotiations. In the end, we asked the Chinese to come up with a suitable reactor design, which the United States, co-chairing the effort, would review and approve.

Another benefit of a free flow of ideas is that a person's ideas often reveal their primary concerns. Every proposal to the group contains more than a little self-interest; by entertaining many ideas, a leader of a negotiation can get some insight into what each party's concerns really are.

◇◇◇◇◇◇◇◇◇◇

I find that coming to consensus tends to require a place—a physical clearinghouse where all ideas are kept and evaluated. Even with all of our whiz-bang satellite communication devices, an ordinary white-board turned out to be the humble lynchpin to our understanding of the Iran deal. We first adopted it at the Beau-Rivage Palace Hotel in Lausanne as we were struggling to agree on the Joint Comprehensive Plan of Action parameters in March 2015. The Iranians had been reluctant since the beginning of the talks to commit any current status of the agreement to paper, since anything set down in black and white, if it got back to Tehran, would constrain their negotiators' ability to explain their positions to their various home constituencies.

One night, realizing that it was past time to get the deal in front of us in writing, I asked my team to find me a very large whiteboard on wheels. Sitting then with Araghchi and Ravanchi and a couple of members of my team, I printed every element of the agreement on the board, and we began a discussion of where we stood on each topic and where the Iranians stood. We all furiously took notes, and by the end of the discussion we had the information needed to negotiate. Then, for secrecy's sake, and to affirm that nothing discussed had formal standing, we erased the whiteboard.

The whiteboard became so valuable that I had its diagram of all the elements transferred to paper so that Secretary Kerry could carry around with him a complete map of those elements. The technical team also began using the whiteboard in no-fault discussions with other delegations for calculations of the interlocking pieces of a deal. The whiteboard's importance to the negotiations among our nuclear experts became clear when a member of another team mistakenly used a regular, non-erasable marker. The incident nearly paralyzed the entire negotiation.

The whiteboard, where we could easily smudge out and rewrite, became not only our public square for discussion but a symbol of the overall dynamic of the deal and its intersecting parts. It was during the whiteboard sessions that the adage "Nothing is agreed until everything is agreed" became a truism for the comprehensive deal, as it had been for the interim agreement.

◇◇◇◇◇◇◇◇◇◇

Information-sharing is a norm. So is shared responsibility. We strove to make every delegation part of the broader group effort. This was often challenging with the Chinese, partly because of geographic distance and language, but also because of their diplomatic culture. The Chinese have come a very long way from my early, Clinton-era days at State, when the Chinese delegations constantly had to wait for new talking points from Beijing, which were often delayed because of all the time zones between Beijing and Washington or Europe. By the time of the Iran negotiation, however, the Chinese had put together an expert team with broader authority and a commitment to the deal.

Nonetheless, just as the Russians traditionally defer to the Chinese on matters regarding North Korea, China generally followed the Russians in the Iran negotiations, working closely with them. The Chinese team leader was not their political director, who came only intermittently, but a nuclear nonproliferation specialist who came to the negotiation rounds with a large team. Foreign Minister Wang attended when the other ministers did and worked to bring in Chinese ideas, but it wasn't until the Iranians indicated a preference for the Chinese design to replace the Arak plutonium reactor that they took a larger role, and then only with misgivings: the Chinese were reluctant to take responsibility for a project that would be inspected by the IAEA. The rest of the teams were enthusiastic, since we saw this interest by Iran as a way to gain deeper commitment by the Chinese to the overall deal. Having everyone take on responsibility so as to create joint accountability is a critical norm.

◇◇◇◇◇◇◇◇◇◇◇

Norms are not rules. Norms are for the good of the group, and they apply to everyone equally. Team rules set expectations. They are to be obeyed. They are implicitly hierarchical. When I hire a new person, I like to sit down with them and lay out a few sternly worded rules that are designed in the long run to relieve their stress.

First, if you screw up, own it. Tell me. I hate surprises. I won't embarrass you in front of your colleagues, and I'll help you fix what you've done. But don't make me the last person to know.

Second, be a risk-taker; I'd rather reel you back in from going too far than have to push you out.

Third, know what your role is, and use the power of that role to get what you need, but appreciate that any role has its limits and responsibilities. Respect your colleagues. Help each other out. A little humility goes a long way.

Fourth, stay in touch with my chief of staff or my assistant. They usually know how to solve the unsolvable, and perhaps more importantly, they know what my mood is on any given day!

◇◇◇◇◇◇◇◇◇◇◇

Rules can go up the org chart as well as down. One Sunday afternoon in October 1985, in the small den of the town house I shared with my husband and young daughter in Columbia, Maryland, I found myself on the phone with Barbara Mikulski agreeing to manage her campaign for the US Senate. Two years earlier, as Barbara's chief of staff, I had written a detailed memo that listed some steps she'd have to take if she were ever to run for the Senate. She had taken one of my recommendations nearly immediately—accepting a position as one of several co-chairs of the nascent Mondale presidential campaign. This position allowed her to travel the state and the country to expand her contacts in Maryland outside her Baltimore district and meet the national big-number donors in the Democratic Party that would come in handy for a Senate run. She also took my advice to shift her focus in the House to her assignments on the Energy and Commerce Committee—bread-and-butter areas for the state of Maryland. She'd also begun to pop up more in the national media.

Barbara's efforts had garnered her more than a few mentions around the campaign and in the press as a possible running mate for Mondale. In February, Mondale himself had referred to Barbara at a campaign stop as "the next vice president of the United States." The fireplug, four-foot-eleven Baltimorean wasn't the same vice presidential package as the other names being bandied about—Representative Pat Schroeder of Colorado; Dianne Feinstein, then mayor of San Francisco; or Mondale's eventual pick, New York congresswoman Geraldine Ferraro. Barbara also knew that she was too radical and outspoken to be a safe choice for the second spot on the ticket. I was with her the summer evening she took herself out of the running, using an appearance with Texas governor Ann Richards on *Nightline*. Discussing with Ted Koppel whether this was the year the Democrats would pick a woman for the ticket, Barbara deftly used the spotlight to stand down from her own interests and announce that she was backing Gerry Ferraro for veep. We then flew overnight to the National Organization for Women convention under way in Miami and helped make that happen.

A year later, Barbara was ready to step out on her own, and she'd come knocking, asking me to execute the rest of my memo.

I'd never run a campaign before. At the time my total electoral experience was stuffing envelopes for Lyndon Johnson in Baltimore when I was fifteen, briefly volunteering for Eugene McCarthy and George McGovern, and helping Barbara as a Mondale-Ferraro co-chair. But I felt as if I could do the job if I had some guarantees that it wouldn't ruin my life in the process. I intuitively understood that a leader can't lead without taking care of herself first.

So I set some rules for Barbara. I told her that I needed three things to survive the demands of a campaign. One, she could never call me at the time I usually put my daughter to bed, barring a genuine crisis, and I wouldn't miss bedtime for campaign events unless there was important business being conducted beyond handshakes and a speech. I had quit my job as Barbara's chief of staff because I had a two-year-old whom I wanted to see grow up and a marriage I wanted to keep.

Second, I wanted to be in on every decision. The media and polling consultants could talk with her, at least initially, only when I was present. She was the candidate and would have input on politics, schedule, and media, but our advisory team and the campaign plan would drive the decisions. This wasn't my attempt at micromanaging so much as an effort to ensure that Barbara didn't. We needed the candidate to use her time and talent in ways that none of the rest of us could—on the campaign trail meeting with voters, not in the office debating campaign plans.

Finally, I asked her to give me a list of five friends I could call when I needed someone to take her out for a cup of coffee and leave me the space and time to do the work.

She agreed, and to her credit, she followed the rules, most of the time. If anyone struggled with my campaign-life balance, it was me. There were days when I stomped around the house saying, "I can't do this!," and then, after getting a decent night's sleep, did it anyway. Three days before the Tuesday primary, asking myself what kind of mother shirks her own child's birthday for her job, I threw a birthday party for Sarah, who was turning three. To make sure nobody missed how dutiful I was being, I invited sixteen other three-year-olds and for good measure a clown they had little interest in watching. The day of the party I felt like my head was going to explode.

I knew at the time it was guilt that was driving this particular insanity, and I should have scaled the party back to something more manageable and dealt with my feelings. A wise therapist once told me that no one dies of a little guilt. Since then, whenever I find myself overcompensating, I've tried to remember that line.

◇◇◇◇◇◇◇◇◇◇

When people ask me how I assemble a team, I don't think they expect me to talk about norms and rules and the benefits of skeptics. They don't recognize that my training is in social work, studying the psychology of groups, and that how a team works together is as important to me as who is on it. They want to hear about how I compile the component parts, as if teams were clocks instead of living organisms. Certainly, I value differing skill sets and have no choice, when charged with convincing a country to stop manufacturing nuclear weapons, but to look for people with particular expertise. But I often say that I have always been a social worker, even as my caseload changed from children to politics to diplomacy. The requirements for all three are much the same. ("Politics is social work with power," is Barbara Mikulski's definition.)

Conceiving of teams as the right pieces instead of the right process is a trap: thinking you know the type of person you are looking for prevents you from evaluating people for their skills or expertise. I don't let myself get distracted by my prior notions of who can fill a role or how. When I began negotiating with the Iranians in 2011, the superb nuclear expert on our team was Bob Einhorn, whom I'd worked with on Bill Perry's North Korean review. Frustrated by the Ahmadinejad administration's intransigence and thinking that the effort had become hopeless, Bob left government altogether before Rouhani's election broke the logjam. I recruited our old Perry process colleague Jim Timbie to replace him. The two men could not have been more different—Bob was a political appointee, after years as a civil servant, who easily spoke up in meetings, while Jim was quiet and patient, a State Department lifer who in nearly forty-five years had had a hand in every major and minor arms-control and nuclear negotiation. Despite his reserve, Jim's experience allowed him to play the role of the elder statesman whom no younger member of the team could challenge but who also wanted to encourage younger team members. Switching from Bob to Jim was a reminder that skills outweigh nearly everything else when it comes to filling a job on a team.

The best example of this was one of the first hires I ever made. When I became director of child welfare in Maryland, I desperately needed to hire an executive assistant. Everyone recommended a young woman who, I was astonished to find when I met her, was nearly seven months pregnant. I objected to the veterans who were touting her that I needed help navigating my new position in an agency I'd never set foot in before. How could this woman help me when she planned to take a three-month maternity leave almost as soon as I showed up? My colleagues assured me that she could set up all the systems before she left and would be ready to dig in when she returned. Putting my trust in her would earn her loyalty and hard work.

I was very unsure, but in the end I hired her, and they were absolutely right. She was a talented young woman, and her skills were only enhanced by the respect I earned by accommodating her life and career plans. I also learned a meaningful lesson about the importance of supporting women who want to become mothers and men who want to be fathers: doing what you can to support work-life integration is not just a legal requirement but crucial to having the best employees.

Since then, I try never to let a valuable person's needs deter me from hiring them. When I was working for the Democratic National Committee in 1988, I needed to hire an issues person—a policy expert who would oversee the shop that pushed out research papers and statistical support on the issues that crop up during a campaign. Everyone I consulted recommended a Hill aide named Jack Lew, who had worked for Speaker of the House Tip O'Neill. I interviewed him and thought he was fantastic, but as I offered him the job he stopped me. "I want to make sure you understand," he said. "I'm an Orthodox Jew. If you add up the Jewish High Holidays, plus all the Saturdays in September and October between now and the election in November, my religion is going to sideline me for something like half the remaining time in the campaign."

I let him finish before asking him one question. "Can you do what I need you to do?" He didn't pause. "Yes," he answered. "Then let's do it," I said. He was brilliant. In the years after the campaign, Jack did two tours as director of the Office of Management and Budget, putting the budget in balance for the first time in thirty years under President Clinton and returning to serve under President Obama. In 2013, he became secretary of the Treasury. I got a chance to be a part of his stellar career by being flexible about how he got the job done.

After you've built a team, being flexible is also paramount when running it. You should keep an eye out for ways to move people into different roles as they grow and their expertise deepens, or if your needs or theirs suddenly change. My first deputy on the Iran nego-tiation was Brooke Anderson, a former chief of staff for the National Security Council and then deputy UN ambassador, and one of the brightest minds in Washington. She had married and moved to Boze-man, Montana, to live with her husband, but I dragooned her to take up residence in Brussels, where she served as our eyes and ears on the EU's deliberations as well as my deputy on the negotiating team. When she prevailed on us to let her go back to Bozeman, I pointed out to Secretary Kerry and Susan Rice that, if we closed the Iran deal, as was looking likely, we still had to plan for implementation. The only person to write a plan was Brooke, who knew the deal, knew the elements, and knew the team. She recruited her implementation team from the understudies for those at the negotiation table and put out a masterful plan, working remotely from Bozeman and traveling to Washington as needed.

Brooke's replacement as my deputy, meanwhile, was Rob Malley, the senior National Security Council official who supported me down the stretch of the Iran deal. I had a couple of motives in picking Rob. When he had joined the negotiation for a day or two here and there, I had noticed that he was able to pick up the phone and speak directly to National Security Adviser Susan Rice. As we negotiated the last critical points of the deal, experience told me, I'd want to keep the White House informed on a moment-to-moment basis and get answers from them just as quickly. Rob could be that instant conduit to Rice and the president. The NSC officer responsible for the entire Middle East, Rob had plenty on his plate already, so getting Susan to release him was tough. She gave in only after ordering more secure equipment to our quarters in Vienna so that Rob could do both his Washington and Vienna jobs.

Bringing Rob on shows the value of adding specific expertise at critical moments. One morning in February 2014, I was headed to the White House for a principals' meeting to discuss the state of the Iran negotiations when I got an email on my BlackBerry from Abbas Araghchi, the lead negotiator for Iran, saying that Dr. Ali Salehi was going to join the Iranian negotiating team for the upcoming round in Lausanne.

This was a bit of a surprise: Salehi was a big gun, and I immediately wondered why he was being added to the team. We later surmised that Zarif, who had taken a potential technical solution on centrifuges back to Tehran for approval only to have it promptly nixed, saw the wisdom of having a technical expert with political juice on his team. Salehi, head of Iran's Atomic Energy Organization and a vice president of Iran, was the logical choice.

I understood that we had to answer and ensure that we had our own cabinet-level nuclear expert to go head to head with Salehi or everyone would lose face—never a good negotiating posture. When I walked into the Situation Room, I immediately related Abbas's news to Secretary Kerry and Susan Rice. Virtually simultaneously, we all said, "Ernie Moniz"—the secretary of energy, who was Salehi's counterpart in our government. At that moment, Moniz entered the room. "Have we got weekend plans for you," we told him.

In a strange turn, Zarif's gambit in bringing in Salehi ended up as an advantage for the United States. Ernie was a brilliant nuclear physicist who could talk in plain English about complicated issues and had a fondness for a strong scotch before dinner. He quickly became indispensable. Though he protested after each negotiating session that he was no longer needed, we ignored him. He proved a valuable, indispensable, not-so-secret weapon straight through to the selling of the deal to Congress.

◇◇◇◇◇◇◇◇◇◇

Sometimes in assembling a team, you just get lucky. When I set out to get Barbara Mikulski elected to the Senate, I was lucky to have an experienced group of advisers, led by campaign chair Rick Berndt, partner in the prominent Baltimore law firm Gallagher, Evelius and Jones; and Jim Smith, the owner of Subway franchises in the area. Both men had been deeply involved in Senator Paul Sarbanes's winning campaigns and knew everyone in Maryland politics. Bob Shrum and David Doak became our media consultants and Harrison Hickman our pollster, all veterans of many successful Senate campaigns.

The rest of my team I gathered based on favors and hunches. With no money, I had no other choice. My first call that October Sunday evening was to Nikki Heidepriem, a South Dakota–born lawyer I'd met while barnstorming with Barbara on the Mondale-Ferraro campaign. Smart and a savvy lawyer, Nikki had been in charge of organizing women nationally for Mondale. If Barbara was to win, we would need women. Barbara would be the first Democratic woman elected to the US Senate in her own right, a fact that I knew would inspire the state's female voters. Nikki knew how to organize them. I told Nikki that I needed a communications director, a job she'd never done before, and offered her $3,000 a month, out of funds I didn't yet have. Fortunately, she said yes, and we dove in together.

Over the next weeks we found a storefront campaign headquarters on Charles Street in downtown Baltimore, all of it open space save for a small enclosure in the back that I would claim for my office. Volunteers handled most everything at first—women did indeed flock to support Barbara, adding to her cadre of devoted supporters from her congressional campaigns and community organizing. Meanwhile, I set about hiring paid staff. I wish I could claim credit for the team I built, but the truth is that some of the best simply walked in off the street and into our campaign.

One of those finds was a young guy fresh off Gary Hart's presidential campaign named Martin O'Malley, just the gutsy field organizer the campaign needed. Martin, who would go on to be Baltimore's mayor, then Maryland governor and ultimately a presidential candidate, was still at the University of Maryland law school at the time, though he admitted that he had all but stopped showing up for class. A hunk who played in an Irish rock band, he was a favorite among young women voters (despite his nasty habit of chewing tobacco) and a precociously brash figure among the hard-bitten pols of Maryland politics. Better yet, he came from Montgomery County, near DC—I didn't want everyone on the campaign to be from Baltimore. Since he was a Hart person, I could count on him to draw other Hart people to a staff full of Mondale supporters. Not least, Martin, who was desperate to get into politics and just needed to attach himself to a winner, was willing to be paid very little.

Like Martin, Lucie Lehmann was a walk-on who showed up at our office one day to interview for a fundraising position. Raised in Switzerland, Lucie had a European style that was a hit with donors, and she was relentless in pursuit of money. She became the fundraiser who never let me down.

It was a team whose passion far outpaced their experience, but we prospered on the strength of their hard work and our naturally gifted candidate—and did I mention luck? Our phones were answered by a volunteer named Mike Morrell, who would rise to become Mikulski's state director. One day Morrell called back to my office that Warren Beatty was on hold. I said, "Excuse me?" I got on the phone. Beatty, who had been raised in Virginia, had come to visit his father, who was recuperating from an illness at Johns Hopkins Medical Center in Baltimore. He asked me if there was anything he could do for Barbara. It so happened that we had a fundraiser that night. We added Beatty to the roster of speakers, and Mikulski and he did a funny set-to with each other. It showed me how you can never tell what's going to happen in the course of a campaign.

Barbara caught fire with voters with her unvarnished progressivism and her fresh turns of phrase. She handily beat her primary opponents, a sitting governor and a popular Montgomery County congressman, then invited voters to come back for the general election by telling them not to make their support "a one-night stand." They complied, and in the general Barbara dispatched Republican Linda Chavez, a former Reagan administration official, in a state Reagan had swept with 58 percent of the vote two years earlier.

Barbara's campaign taught me a lot about myself as a leader of a team. The fact is, I am better at building institutions than at maintaining them; these tasks are actually quite different. I am like a campaign junkie—signing on for the rush of the election season, which has a beginning, a middle, and an end in the space of a year or so, and then moving on to the next one when it's over.

My desire for change can sometimes get me in trouble. In 1986, after shepherding Barbara to her Senate victory, I decided to return to Maryland state government to become special secretary for children and youth as part of Governor Donald Schaefer's cabinet. A wonderful activist for children named Theresa Landsberg had convinced Schaefer that he needed someone like me, but neither she nor Schaefer had thought through what the job was. A bigger problem, however, was that I missed being involved in national politics and national issues. I had been swimming in the big pond for five years. The smaller pond of state government felt too restricting. The pace was slower, the stakes different.

I also didn't fit because the job turned out to be concerned greatly with teenagers in crisis. Even seven years after my brother's death, I realized, I wasn't far enough removed emotionally from it to be helpful to others in crisis. I remember giving a speech to folks about at-risk youth and thinking the whole time about my brother. I gave the speech but knew I couldn't stay. It wasn't that I lacked skills or dedication to the cause, but that I couldn't give myself to the job.

The worst part may have been telling the governor. Schaefer was a sometimes-brusque figure who had devoted his life fully to Maryland politics, first as a beloved tough-love mayor of Baltimore, then as governor of the state. He's not the kind of guy you quit on. Nonetheless, I showed up for my one-on-one in his office in Annapolis, with its incongruous masses of delicate African violets, and told him I was going back to Washington. He wasn't happy, and that conversation was one of the most difficult in my professional career. But I left his office feeling free again, the best indication that I'd done the right thing.

In all that I do, I have to know that I have a real role on the team. In 1989, after Mike Dukakis's loss to George H. W. Bush, I left the DNC and took Ellen Malcolm up on a long-standing offer to be executive director of the organization she founded, EMILY's List. I had introduced Ellen to Barbara Mikulski four years before, just as Barbara was beginning her campaign for Senate. Running against two deeply connected Democratic men in the primary, Barbara had to put up a big number in her first official fundraising report to the Federal Election Commission, to show that we were a force to be reckoned with. So I put in a call to Ellen, whom I knew through mutual friends, and over lunch in the House dining room it was decided that Barbara would become EMILY's List's banner candidate.

I believed deeply in the organization, not only because, as Mikulski's campaign manager, I would benefit directly from its support, but because it was an ingenious and generous innovation—not words you hear too much of in American politics. In 1985, working with a small group of like-minded friends, Ellen, a longtime anonymous donor to progressive causes, realized that lack of campaign money was a major barrier to women's campaign success, so she began EMILY's List in order to fund the campaigns of pro-choice Democratic women. Ellen rightly posited that if an organization could promote and bundle money in the early stages for promising candidates, more money would follow on—EMILY stood for "Early Money Is Like Yeast," which "makes the dough rise." The group even adopted the red and yellow colors that adorn Fleischmann's-brand yeast packets. Ellen had also prepared herself with more than a great idea and personal wealth: she had gone out and earned an MBA.

An early effort to help Harriet Woods in Missouri become that first Democratic woman to be elected in her own right did not quite get over the line, but EMILY's List's support of Mikulski in Maryland made history. Both of Barbara's opponents in the primary had access to deep financial wells. Governor Hughes had been a statewide candidate twice before; Congressman Barnes could draw on his district in the wealthy Washington suburbs. EMILY's List was an important resource for us. When the first fundraising reports came out, much to the shock of Mikulski's competitors, she matched them in dollars, and the race was on.

After I joined EMILY's List in 1989, we set our sights on increasing the paltry number of Democratic women in the House of Representatives. Looking for areas where redistricting had erased a seat and taken away a congressman's incumbency advantage, we identified Democratic women whom we felt we could train to run. We enlisted the help of Gwen Margolis, a Democratic state senator who was leading the redistricting effort in Florida, and we canvassed her state for up-and-comers who had a chance to run and win—women like Carrie Meek and Lois Frankel. We undertook similar strategies in other states, like California, where we backed Anna Eshoo, a San Mateo board supervisor who had lost her bid for Congress in the previous cycle. In 1992, she won a seven-way primary and the seat. She has served the heart of Silicon Valley ever since and been a member of the Democratic leadership team in the House for more than a decade.

This tedious and painstaking redistricting and training work, with an enormous response by EMILY's List members, decidedly helped make 1992 the so-called Year of the Women: four Democratic women senators and twenty Democratic women House members were sworn in. It's hard to put into context today how extraordinary this effort was, especially in this era before the internet, when everything had to be done by mail. Work on state-level politics meant getting on airplanes and spending time on the ground, driving around to meet talented women who didn't even know yet that they would run for Congress. Developing people, helping them realize their best selves, while also advancing a political agenda you believe in, is a great high.

But EMILY's List was above all Ellen Malcolm. She was the engine that drove a groundbreaking effort, and she is a hero who has made many women well known for their service while remaining largely unknown and unsung herself. Ellen Malcolm, in sum, *was* EMILY's List. She had hired me because she wanted to step back from the day-to-day operation, but when it came to really letting go, she left very little space for me to do more and I became a woman without a role. As difficult as it was to leave, given the mission of EMILY's List and my affection and respect for Ellen, I knew myself well enough to know that I needed space to grow professionally. After two exciting and successful years, I moved on, looking for a team that would make the most of my skills, something that would demand similar dogged persistence and have a similar, if not even greater, purpose.

chapter six

PERSISTENCE

In late March 2015, the enormous traveling show that the Iran talks had become arrived in Lausanne, the picturesque Swiss city on Lake Geneva. We were now four months past our latest blown deadline, and we were already bearing down on the last day of June, the new deadline we'd set for ourselves to get the deal done. The press trailed our every move in and out of the beautiful Beau-Rivage Palace, another historic nineteenth-century hotel. Coco Chanel had lived there for a time—one of her dogs, it was said, was buried somewhere on the grounds, but I never came across the gravesite.

More apt, I thought, was the giant chessboard laid out behind one of the wings of the hotel, complete with chest-high chess pieces. The issues we had to settle in the next few days had fallen into stalemate over what would trigger the lifting of the economic sanctions. Would they be removed once we signed the deal, or when it had been verified that the Iranians were in compliance? Other outstanding issues concerned the low-enriched uranium the Iranians were holding—would they have to ship it to a third country or could they sell it on the open market?—and how much access the International Atomic Energy Agency would get to their military bases. And as always, one central question remained unanswered: how many centrifuges would the Iranians get to keep spinning?

We'd given ourselves a week in Lausanne to figure all of this out, thinking we'd then have all of April and May to finally put everything that we agreed on into a single document that the P5+1 nations and Iran could sign off on. We planned all this in full recognition of the fact that we hadn't met one of our self-imposed deadlines yet.

As the talks started, the Iranians agreed to some important points, but in the following days they reopened the bidding on those same points. The march toward an agreement suddenly seemed to stall. We'd wrap up one meeting feeling as if we'd made strides, only to find in the next meeting that we'd made no progress at all. Anything that looked like closure was immediately suspect.

To us, it looked like the Iranians were purposely wasting our time, perhaps buying themselves room for their illicit activities. Time was a constant worry for us too, because the longer the deal took, the more political pressure we felt. And it didn't help when both Democrats and Republicans at home seemed to suspect that we were rushing to make the deal work and began counseling us on the Sunday talk shows to slow down.

Our attitude struck the Iranians as a confidence gap, which in turn made them uneasy. "We have a very serious problem of confidence," they told reporters at one point at the Beau-Rivage, "a mutual lack of confidence we need to address."

As the week came to an end and our latest deadline expired, Kerry got so frustrated that he went to see Zarif alone in his hotel suite. Not for the last time, he gave the Iranian foreign minister an ultimatum that basically said, as I recall, if you can't do this deal, if you're not serious, go back to Tehran and get some instructions!

On April 1, we sat down at nine o' clock in the evening, after breaking into smaller groups for dinner. We didn't leave the table until nearly dawn, at which point we were at such loggerheads, and so spent, that we agreed to break. I got to sleep around 7:00 in the morning, woke up shortly thereafter to have some breakfast with strong Swiss coffee, and got back to the table about 9:30. As we pushed past the last few roadblocks, the adrenaline of getting closer kept us going. By the early afternoon of April 2, we had hammered out a framework that we could all live with.

Hours later, surrounded by all of the ministers, Zarif and Federica Mogherini, the EU's new high representative, replacing Cathy Ashton, announced our progress. Only two days late. The parameters for a complete deal had come together in greater detail than anyone had expected. I can still remember the smiles of the principals on the dais and the pops of the photographers' cameras coming faster than champagne bubbles.

Then the wheels came off again. A week after our triumph in Lausanne, Supreme Leader Ali Khamenei gave a speech to a handpicked audience of dignitaries in Tehran in which he appeared not to recognize any of the parameters we'd just agreed to. "Nothing has been done yet," Khamenei said flatly. Instead of echoing the show-me standard we'd agreed to in Lausanne, the ayatollah demanded that sanctions be lifted as soon as a deal was signed. He seemed to say too that the IAEA would not be going anywhere near Iranian military sites.

Rubbing salt in the wound, Khamenei followed with a tweet tarring the United States as double-dealers. Americans, he wrote, "always deceive & breach promises."

The Supreme Leader's speech was just a start. For the next six months, the Iran talks bumped from one crisis to another, and more than once threatened to break up entirely.

Diplomacy is not for the faint of heart. "Soft power," as it is sometimes referred to in Washington lately, isn't really soft at all. Practiced correctly, it is tough and smart, and it is guaranteed to be difficult. It ebbs and flows, has good days and bad, and rarely achieves its objectives in a linear fashion. One can't be in a rush. The details must be precise and the language correct, since the words you agree to will be interpreted and reargued by both sides as they carry out the terms amid the jostle of events. Enforcement must be clear and consequences spelled out for all.

Sometimes, it's true, diplomacy turns into a race—for instance, when an emergency, like the Syrians' use of chemical weapons, demands an instant response to save lives or to stave off military repercussions. Most days, however, diplomacy is a slog, and one of the primary requirements of negotiation is the persistence to continue to get the job done, and then go back and do it again when human nature inevitably causes your bulwark to crumble.

Negotiation is a spiritual and intellectual struggle as well as a physical one. Apart from the mental endurance needed to keep manifold technical details and organizational steps in mind at once, there are the draining routines of airports and hotels—even luxury suites lose their charm when laundry must be hand-washed and hung around the bathroom and thrice-daily meetings produce enough printer paper and snack bags to rival a campaign headquarters on election night. You work through bad colds, the flu, stomach bugs, and even broken fingers.

In the fall of 2013, I rushed out of a briefing on the Iran deal for US senators in their secure meeting room, on my way to another briefing for House members. As I skipped down a circular staircase in the bowels of the Capitol, my right hand on the banister, I stumbled and fell forward, forgetting to remove my hand. When I'd steadied myself, I looked down to see that the second joint of my right pinkie finger was perpendicular to the rest of my fingers. Later I would learn that I had suffered a "boutonnière rupture" of the pinkie tendon, which keeps the finger on straight. The sight of my bent finger was disconcerting. The pain was spectacular.

With a machismo born of necessity, I calmly asked a member of State's legislative affairs team to find me some ice and continued to the House briefing. When the ice pack arrived, I plopped my hand on it and proceeded to give what was probably the most focused briefing of my life, trying hard to ignore the glowing pain in my hand. When the briefing ended, Republican representative Ed Royce, the California congressman who chaired the House Foreign Affairs Committee, came to the witness table to offer his thanks. In reply, I burst into tears. Royce whisked me through the basement network to the House physician, who sent me to the emergency room at George Washington University Hospital.

The next day I sat in an orthopedic surgeon's examination room, listening to him recommend surgery, though during postsurgical recovery my hand would be unusable for weeks. In that case, I told him, surgery was not an option. The Iranians had just begun to negotiate in earnest, and we were finally making unprecedented progress on a possible deal. For one thing, I needed my right hand so I could take notes at the negotiation table. But I also couldn't imagine giving up crucial days to recuperation and physical therapy. I convinced the orthopedist to limit my treatment to a series of splints that would allow me to avoid surgery. To this day my crooked little finger is a permanent reminder of that day, and the little sacrifices we make to achieve great things.

Nine months later, at the negotiation at the Coburg in Vienna, I was racing to keep an appointment for a secure phone call with Secretary Kerry in our delegation's suite on the hotel's top floor—a beautiful aerie that had been cleared of its sumptuous furniture to make room for work tables and modern and secure communications equipment. The room had a dedicated elevator, which, responding to a swipe from a special key, took you up and opened onto a foyer and a set of glass doors that were normally left open. That night someone had closed them. In my haste, I took no notice and smashed into the thick glass at the speed of someone running to get a ringing phone. Seeing me bleeding profusely, my male colleagues yelled to call an ambulance, but I stopped them. "Clearly none of you are mothers" were my exact words. I did ask for ice (again), which I held to my nose for the duration of the call without letting on to Secretary Kerry that something was amiss. He didn't find out about my collision with the door until months later.

This time the doctor surprised me by taking my injury in stride. A well-known nose-and-throat specialist who attended to the famous opera singers who regularly swung through Vienna, he greeted me in English, saying of my banged-up face, "Shit happens."

My nose, it turned out, was broken in more than one place, but perhaps because he was used to the diplomatic types who frequent Vienna, the doctor knew I would make the negotiations my priority.

He packed my nose, **wrote** me a handful of prescriptions, and sent me on my way. I soon removed the packing and then used heavy makeup to cover most of the black, blue, and subsequently green and purple bruises. Most of my colleagues from other countries never knew any better, and the American team didn't miss a beat.

With everyone from Kerry to Salehi suffering through worse ailments, I was not going to let a couple of orthopedic mishaps stop me. Anyway, physical maladies were the least of it. It was heartache that could really get us down. As the negotiation sessions commonly went on for hours and days beyond expectations and the talks themselves went months past even our extended deadlines, children had birthdays without parents on hand, funerals were held, family vacations were postponed, and marriages felt the strain of absence. Essential team members had to leave because of economic and family circumstances. Hundreds of thousands of miles were flown, hundreds of hours of sleep were missed, and more schnitzel was eaten than I imagined possible.

◇◇◇◇◇◇◇◇◇◇

Persistence is not synonymous with patience. Though a negotiator is often required to reset calmly and keep going, at times it's more efficient to let the anger flow. After the ayatollah reset his "red lines" for the nuclear deal in his Tehran speech following the Lausanne meetings, we initially dismissed the purported change of course, presuming that he was speaking for the benefit of the most conservative factions in his government. If the talks failed, we imagined, he'd need cover to blame the United States for asking too much, in keeping with the Iranian party line. President Obama, speaking to reporters on a trip to Cuba, coolly explained, "Even a guy with the title 'Supreme Leader' has to be concerned about his own constituencies."

Privately, however, we were livid, especially after Zarif, who had agreed to everything we'd released after Lausanne, fell in line with the ayatollah's disavowals. He tweeted, and then repeated on Iranian television, the contention that the parameters of the interim deal that the White House had issued after Lausanne were "in contradiction" to the new framework.

At the next bilateral negotiating session, in Geneva in late May, we found Zarif unrepentant. At one point in the middle of a six-hour meeting, with progress not coming easily, the foreign minister retreated from the table, his head in his hands. Releasing his own frustration, Secretary Kerry slammed his fist down on the table so hard that the pen he was holding catapulted across the table and hit Abbas Araghchi. The rest of us at the table froze for a moment, terrified because Kerry so rarely lost his temper, and because physical violence, even an inadvertent flip of a pen, is unheard of in diplomatic exchanges. Kerry quickly apologized for the accident, Araghchi demurred, and the tough discussion continued, if a bit more circumspectly.

In diplomacy, you can't rely on intimidation or exasperation. A good shouting match can sometimes dislodge one side or the other from an untenable position, but drama can also waste valuable time. Besides, not everything that goes wrong is the result of strategic or simple bloody-minded intransigence. About the time Kerry's pen flew across the table, the technical side of the talks, which had been going so well since Ernie Moniz had linked up with Ali Salehi, had nearly come to a standstill as Salehi suddenly disappeared from the talks. Though the Iranians were never clear about why he'd left, we later surmised that his absence was due to a colonoscopy that had led to difficult surgery. We could have shouted all we liked, but there was nothing to do but wait for him to recover and return to the table.

There were several times when I thought that there was no way forward and that we'd have to go back to the president and the American people and explain that we'd failed. In dark moments like these, I look for any thread of agreement that will pull a negotiation forward again and try to remember what dug me out of the last bleak moment. In the Iran negotiations, we had plenty of those dark moments to choose from. It was always instructive for me to remember that the outreach to Iran itself was the best example of persistence we could name. The first, delicate seeds of the Iran deal were sown in the aftermath of President Bush's 2002 State of the Union Address, when he had called Iraq, North Korea, and Iran the "axis of evil"— not exactly an opening bid for an international agreement. Not long afterward, the Iranian ambassador to the United Nations had reached out to try to establish a back channel to the United States. It was rebuffed by the Bush administration, but John Kerry, then chair of the Senate Foreign Relations Committee, took notice of that ambassador as a forward-thinker among the Iranian elite, and someone with whom he could deal. Of course, that man was Javad Zarif.

When bulling your way forward doesn't work, your best option may be to take a flyer—float an outlandish idea in hopes that its sheer bravado will clear everyone's minds. At the worst, it may spur discussion; at best, it can be the solution everyone else has been secretly hoping for. That's precisely what happened after Syria perpetrated a horrific chemical weapons attack on its own people at Ghouta in August 2013.

Carried out by the Syrian Air Force under the orders of President Bashar Al-Assad, the attack on Ghouta provoked an immediate international crisis. Assad's considerable supply of chemical weapons had been one of the most vexing issues in the world's attempts to calm Syria's civil war. Ghouta wasn't the first time Assad had used those weapons against his own people. A year earlier, President Obama had told the American press at a White House briefing that he considered the use of chemical weapons a "red line" that Assad would be wise not to cross. Ever since his warning, we'd been stumped as to how to get control of Assad's store of weapons.

Now reports were coming in, backed up by YouTube videos and corroborated by Doctors Without Borders, that Assad had crossed the red line. Obama was expected to order airstrikes at any minute on Assad's weapons depots, and potentially on ground troops in Syria. The Russians, who backed Assad, were watching closely. What had been mostly an internal fight was threatening to become a proxy war between American and Russian forces.

At the State Department, those of us on the seventh floor, the secretary's floor, were completely absorbed by the crisis. We met almost continuously, with large groups convened in the secretary's conference room and more impromptu gatherings in his private office. Certainly, most of us believed that we should strike Syria without much more ado. We were immensely proud when, on a Friday afternoon a week after Ghouta, Secretary Kerry delivered a passionate speech setting out, we thought at the time, the definitive prestrike rationale.

Then the world—and all of us—seemed to hold its breath. By Saturday afternoon, there was no airstrike. Obama had decided to go to Congress for authorization. Many of us, knowing he would not get it (Obama knew this too), were devastated that he chose not to follow up on his red line, even understanding the circumstances.

The next week, at a press conference in London, where Kerry was meeting with the British government on Syria, he was asked what Assad could do to avoid an attack. He appeared to shrug off the question as fantasy. "He could turn over every single bit of his chemical weapons to the international community in the next week," the secretary said. He threw up his hands, as if he'd tossed away his own suggestion as soon as he'd made it. "All of it," he continued, "without delay, and allow a full and total accounting before that. But he isn't about to do it, and it can't be done."

And with that he went on to the next question. Later that day the official State Department line was that the secretary's scenario was "a rhetorical argument."

But in Moscow, the Russian foreign minister, Sergey Lavrov, was listening, and chose to run with it. In short order, Lavrov announced that he had spoken to the Syrians about just such a deal. He proposed that Assad's declared chemical weapons be inventoried and then shipped to Russia to be destroyed. Very quickly, the Russian news agency Interfax released a statement from the Syrian side. "The Syrian Arab Republic welcomed the Russian initiative, based on the concerns of the Russian leadership for the lives of our citizens and the security of our country." Shortly thereafter, United Nations secretary-general Ban Ki-moon weighed in affirmatively.

Whether Kerry had been serious or not, an agreement was suddenly coming together, seemingly out of thin air.

At the time, I was still getting to know John Kerry, with whom I had gotten off to a bit of a bumpy start. When he took over as secretary in February after President Obama's reelection in 2012, I had no idea whether he would keep me on as undersecretary for political affairs. I was a Hillary Clinton hire, and, in the ways of

Washington, my job was to help him settle in until such time as he found his own political director to replace me. In my first meeting with him in his office at State, I recall saying precisely that—that I was glad to help him settle in. In Kerry's recollection, I did more than hope. He maintains that in that first interview I thanked him for keeping me on. He didn't really object—he'd planned to let me continue—but he remembers finding my assumption that he would keep me a trifle presumptuous. We still jokingly disagree about it to this day.

Whatever was said, when the chemical weapons fell on Ghouta, I became Kerry's "wingman," to use his term, in the negotiations with Russia. A negotiation team had to be assembled quickly, and travel orders needed to be written, equipment organized, and background papers written. These tasks normally fall to the executive secretary of the State Department, along with the undersecretary for management, who gets it all organized. But it was apparent in the aftershock of the Syrian chemical attacks that Kerry also needed someone to lead the team on the ground during the actual negotiations, ensuring that all of the moving parts were understood and fit together to meet American interests. As the members of the team gathered for their marching orders, I went to Kerry's chief of staff, David Wade, and offered to take on the role, and he and Kerry quickly accepted that offer. Soon we were all off to Geneva.

The next days were jam-packed as subgroups met with their Russian counterparts on various technical matters. We all had to agree on exactly what kinds of chemical weapons Syria had, including precursor chemicals and ingredients. Other subgroups worked on how to transport the weapons and chemicals safely, who would do so, and how the workers would be protected, since many of the storage sites were in conflict areas. We had to solve where the weapons would go, how and where they would be destroyed, how the process would be monitored, and of course, who would pay for it.

My job was to keep track of these issues and make sure they were resolved in ways that were in the interest of the United States. In any discussion as technical and scientific as chemical weapons, the experts inevitably hit political roadblocks, at which point folks like me and, more importantly, the secretary of state and the foreign minister needed to get involved.

The final negotiation, however, came down to the top diplomats. We met over a small square table by the pool of the Intercontinental Hotel in Geneva, with Secretary Kerry and Foreign Minister Lavrov joined by me and Lavrov's deputy, Sergey Ryabkov, to finalize the details.

The last remaining issue dealt with enforcing Syria's compliance. After hard bargaining, it was agreed that if Syria didn't turn over the chemicals as the deal demanded, their failure to comply would fall under what's called Chapter VII, which allows the UN to respond with sanctions and even military force—with "all necessary means," as the traditional phrase goes. This was the requirement that the United States was looking for. Just days after Kerry took his flier— when he suggested in London that Assad get rid of his chemical weapons—a deal was done. A week later, the agreement, dealing with all declared chemical weapons and their precursors, was approved as United Nations Resolution 2118.

There is another important lesson about persistence that came out of Resolution 2118. A chemical weapons deal with Syria was a huge win. At a time when the United States seemed to respond re-flexively to any problem with military threats, the chemical deal gave promise to the idea that diplomacy, instead of bombs, could lead us out of not only the Syrian troubles but other difficult situations around the globe. It represented a hard turn away from the previous decade of foreign policy in the Middle East, which had emphasized military solutions over political ones.

Today we know that Syria had probably secreted away at least the makings of new weapons, if not the weapons themselves, and that it used those weapons on its own people again. In April 2017, Assad used chemical weapons in the village of Khan Sheikhoun. Many have pointed to that recent attack to say that Resolution 2118 failed its purpose and caused us to drop our vigilance, that given the subsequent attack, the deal was a double failure.

On their face, these arguments are untrue. Resolution 2118 resulted in tons of chemical weapons being taken out of Syria, and Assad learned that he wouldn't be able to use what he had secreted away from our inspectors with impunity. Further attacks were at least delayed. But there is a larger truth about the reality of diplomacy: negotiations are ultimately incremental, and there is no one-size-fits-all solution for all situations. Resolution 2118 solved the problem in front of us in September 2013 but not the problem of Bashar Al-Assad's dictatorship and, as it turns out, his apparent secreting of chemical weapons supplies, all of which demands our attention yet today. That said, an agreement that fixes one problem should not be sacrificed even though other problems remain or arise. Although we always wish that our work will be durable and comprehensive, the results of our efforts are constantly being reshaped by outside events. Each solution is only sufficient to its time and place and the ripeness of a solution.

Military fixes, it should be noted, are no more permanent. World War I, fought as a war to end all wars, resulted in another conflict within twenty years. World War II didn't end conflict in the world— or even, painfully, fascism or anti-Semitism.

◇◇◇◇◇◇◇◇◇◇◇

We need to be able to persist in the face of criticism. Indeed, our ability to persist is tested most when we are criticized by those closest to us. I found this out as a young person working for the University of Southern California's Washington Public Affairs Center, managing community-based mental health grants around the country and teaching USC undergraduates about public policy. One day my boss, Dr. Art Naparstek, who had been an important mentor to me, called me in to talk about a grant proposal I had written. He not only ripped apart the proposal but accused me of not working up to my ability. He ordered me to double down and rewrite the proposal from scratch. I knew he was right substantively but was crushed that I had fallen so far from his good graces.

With the help of a colleague, I rewrote the proposal, but my confidence was deeply shaken. That semester I know I was a lousy teacher, having let the criticism inhabit my whole being. I considered quitting.

Lucky for me, my self-pity was tempered by the need for a paying job. I stuck it out and learned the first lesson of surviving a tough critique. No matter how bad the tongue-lashing, you'll come out the other side and be better prepared to succeed another day.

And no matter how long you work in Washington, you never quite get used to the sharp criticism built into our two-party system. When I was nominated to be the assistant secretary for legislative affairs in 1993, I had to undergo what should have been a fairly routine confirmation hearing in front of the Senate Foreign Relations Committee. The chairman at the time, North Carolina Republican senator Jesse Helms, was a formidable conservative who roundly resented the money and time spent on foreign policy. Anytime he got the chance to rake the State Department over the coals, he took it. So as the nominee of the ambitious new Democratic president, I knew I was facing a rough day at the witness table. To counteract the worst of Helms's purely political enmity, it was suggested that my husband and ten-year-old daughter attend the hearing. The crusty chairman, it was said, had a soft spot for families and children.

What I didn't know was that Senator Helms had spent some time with a conspiratorially conservative book by the investigative reporter David Brock. (Once an erstwhile member of the right wing, Brock has since become a valiant supporter of Hillary Clinton.) In *The Real Anita Hill,* his account of the 1991 confirmation hearings in which Justice Clarence Thomas had faced accusations of sexual harassment, Brock had an account of a weekend two years earlier when I had helped Hill, Thomas's accuser, prepare for her appearance before the Senate Judiciary Committee. Hill's legal team, though first-rate, had little experience with Capitol Hill, so mutual friends had asked me to join the team to help out. I did little in the way of coaching Hill for her testimony; my advice was more in the way of logistics—as basic as how to reserve a room on the Senate side of the Capitol Building to sit in while waiting for the hearing to begin. I also helped her interpret what various senators were asking. Ultimately, Thomas, as we know, was confirmed to the Supreme Court. But Helms had not gotten past the flap. Now, two years after the Thomas-Hill hearings, he faced me down from the dais and asked pointedly if I intended to lie to the Senate in my capacity as legislative affairs director, as I had supported Anita Hill's lies before the Senate.

I took a very deep breath and answered that I did not lie, that I would not lie, and that Anita Hill did not lie. I tried to move the line of attack back toward the question of my competence by adding that I took my constitutional responsibilities seriously. Mostly I was trying not to imagine my daughter listening to a powerful US senator accuse her mother of being a liar.

I went on to have a courteous relationship with Senator Helms and eventually came to be grateful to have endured the hearing, which helped me prepare for the big-league criticism of Washington politics.

The rough-and-tumble of the Hill did not fully prepare me, however, for the criticism I faced during the Iran negotiation. To hear Iranians shouting, "Death to Wendy Sherman," on the streets of Tehran is terrifying in its own way. The Iranians had a way of personalizing the to-and-fro of the talks for their loyal party members that Americans would regard as absurd. Imagine the Young Americans for Freedom marching up Broadway denouncing someone as obscure to most of their fellow citizens as Abbas Araghchi. More disconcerting were the mysterious emails my daughter and I got claiming that my husband was having an adulterous affair in Europe—he wasn't—while I was at the negotiating table. The emails, only about four in total, came about a week before each negotiating round. They ultimately stopped, and I never learned who sent them, but they seemed to be an effort to knock me off balance during the negotiations.

None of the Iranian psy-ops, nor those of other countries, was as hurtful as being called an appeaser in the halls of Congress, which I consider my professional alma mater. Particularly painful, personally, was the mistrust from some members of the Jewish community, at home and abroad, who sat on the far opposite side and could not see the necessity for the deal that I saw.

I wasn't alone in suffering the doubters. President Obama's decision to change the dialogue with Iran had plenty of detractors, as any assault on the status quo always does. The president had to summon the will repeatedly to buck criticism from our allies. Secretary Kerry too had to endure the eloquently blistering misgivings of some former Senate colleagues. Such strong disagreement from people whom I know he respected must have hit him hard.

For purely pragmatic, checks-and-balances reasons, pushing back on the resistance from Congress was our chief concern. The Iran deal would not be submitted as a treaty, which would require sixty votes to win ratification in the Senate. Rather, the deal was classified as an executive action, a prerogative of the executive branch to manage foreign affairs under the power delegated in the Constitution. But Congress had the ability to override any agreement we made on lifting sanctions by passing new ones. As the deal got closer to completion, the members began to make more noise about holding a vote to formally approve or disapprove it, which would not only set up troublesome jurisdictional questions but put the multilateral deal that had been reached at risk.

Members of both parties had legitimate substantive questions about the deal. (The Republican side, in addition, had political reasons for wanting to see it fall apart.) Over the previous four years, I had spent easily a hundred hours or more meeting en masse or one-on-one with members of Congress, keeping them abreast of the talks. I regularly visited the Hill in the company of David Cohen, the undersecretary of the Treasury for terrorism and financial intelligence (until he was made deputy director of the CIA late in the going) and the national intelligence manager for Iran. We'd meet in classified settings with the chairs and ranking members of the key congressional committees—Intelligence, Foreign Relations, Defense, Appropriations, Banking—and the House and Senate leadership.

These two-hour sessions, despite some snickering and name-calling from some of the deal's most dedicated opponents, were draining but worth it. Vocal critics like then-House Majority Leader Eric Cantor asked very thoughtful questions, and Democrats asked some tough ones as well. I give the members great credit. They put in their time understanding how we expected the deal to work, and for the most part they didn't leak.

As we headed to Lausanne to agree on the framework of the Joint Comprehensive Plan of Action (JCPOA), however, the opposition stiffened sharply. The possibility that we might actually succeed in getting an agreement fleshed out seemed to energize Republicans and Israelis. What's more, they began to act in concert to foil the progress being made.

From the beginning of the Obama administration, Israeli prime minister Benjamin Netanyahu had warned that negotiating with Tehran only allowed them time to build up their nuclear capability. From the very beginning of President Obama's overtures to Iran, Netanyahu had argued for solving Iran's push for a bomb with a preemptive military strike. "There's a three-way race going on here," an Obama aide told the *New York Times* in the spring of 2009. "We're racing to make diplomatic progress. The Iranians are racing to make their nuclear capability a fait accompli. And the Israelis, of course, are racing to come up with a convincing military alternative that could plausibly set back the Iranian program."

As the P5+1 talks resumed in the late summer of 2012, Netanyahu used an address to the United Nations General Assembly to turn up the volume on his alarm. He brought to the podium with him a chart illustrated with a cartoonish nuclear bomb purportedly showing that Iran was already less than a year from making enough enriched uranium for a nuclear weapon. (A few weeks later, *Newsweek* reported on a leaked document by the Israeli intelligence agency Mossad that cast severe doubt on the prime minister's timeline.)

As the delegations headed to Lausanne, Netanyahu, who had accepted an invitation by Speaker of the House John Boehner to address the joint houses of Congress, used his March 2015 speech, of course, to denounce the deal. His unprecedented appearance was largely aimed at making Iran an issue for American voters—Netanyahu, who had never gotten on well with President Obama's policies, was implicitly pushing for a party change in the White House, while Boehner was tallying points with American Jews. But coming as we were entering the long homestretch of negotiations on a final agreement, the speech could not but throw a grenade into the process.

Netanyahu's appearance didn't help with Democratic senators and representatives who had significant numbers of Jewish constituents. New York senator Chuck Schumer and Maryland's Ben Cardin never did back the deal (though once the deal was in place, neither wanted to withdraw).

The joint session was only the start of a full-court press to reject the deal. Days after Netanyahu's speech, Arkansas senator Tom Cotton wrote an open letter to the "leaders of the Islamic Republic of Iran," informing them that any agreement made without the approval of Congress would only pertain as long as President Obama was in office. "The next president could revoke such an agreement with the stroke of a pen," the letter read, "and future Congresses could modify the terms...at any time."

The letter, which came out of the blue, was a shock when we first read it. We were experienced enough to know that the old caution about partisan differences ending at the water's edge is honored more in the breach. Still, no one could remember when Congress had so publicly and destructively tried to sandbag the executive branch's foreign policy efforts. One retired US Army general branded the letter "mutinous." The fight for the endgame of the deal was on, before we had even completed it.

I don't think that Cotton, a freshman senator who had fought in Iraq, was making trouble for its own sake. He had clearly put thought into his position, and he truly believed that regime change was the only way to guarantee peace in the Middle East. In my view, however, the lesson of Iraq was that regime change brought terrible, unintended consequences.

Like Cotton, several of our most prominent critics misunderstood a basic rule of diplomacy: you have to deal with things as they are, not as you wish them to be. Had we thought that we could wait out the mullahs until they were deposed or saw sense, of course there would have been no need for a negotiated solution.

In any case, once Cotton's letter was out there, the perfidy of the deal became a Republican article of faith. It didn't matter if you were a true believer like Cotton or simply spoiling for a political fight. Forty-seven Republican senators took it on themselves to sign Cotton's "mutinous" letter.

As it turned out, we used the Cotton letter to our advantage— nothing in diplomacy is wasted. When the Iranians claimed afterward that we were asking too much and that they could never sell the deal at home in Tehran, we reminded them that they were not the only ones taking political risks. "Look at this letter," we said, pointing to the forty-seven names at the bottom of Cotton's missive. "You're always saying we have to help you out or we're not going to be able to get this through. We have our own politics as well. You have to help us out."

◇◇◇◇◇◇◇◇◇◇

With Lausanne and a viable framework a fait accompli, the Republican majority leader, Mitch McConnell—who, as it happens, was in Israel the day the Lausanne framework was completed—raised the question of how Congress would conduct its review of any forthcoming agreement with Iran. To that point, we had largely ignored the question of a congressional approval mechanism. Early on, President Obama had decided that we had enough on our hands without opening the thorny question of legislation about a deal we didn't have in hand. Now, I thought, it was getting very dicey. I picked up the phone and called Denis McDonough, who had become White House chief of staff. I told him I thought the time had come to engage. Denis had already reached the same conclusion. He scheduled an internal meeting to think through our approach.

I joined Secretary Kerry and National Security Adviser Susan Rice, along with the White House's legislative affairs staffers, in Denis's office to agree on what the parameters would be for a potential deal with Congress. We knew that the question of a treaty was still on the table for the Republicans, but we felt that we could fend it off. In recent years, because of the sheer volume of business with other countries, such agreements have come to be preferred over legislatively cumbersome treaties. The fact was that the Senate hadn't agreed to any treaty in the recent past, including a disability treaty advocated by former Republican senator Robert Dole, who had come to the Senate floor in his wheelchair to urge passage.

We had another, more substantive reason for putting the Iran deal forward as an executive agreement. The deal would require constant reviews of Iran's compliance and had to allow enough flexibility to snap back sanctions if Iran didn't keep its promises. It was difficult to build this flexibility into a formal treaty.

My own senator, Maryland's Ben Cardin, was now the ranking member of the Senate Foreign Relations Committee. Cardin was no fan of the agreement, but I'd known his family since I was a kid, and I knew he wouldn't stand in the way of a fair review of the deal.

After the meeting, Denis went to Cardin to negotiate a review process and, largely through Cardin, negotiated a bill with Republican senator Bob Corker, chairman of the Foreign Relations Committee. What we got was a process whereby, if Congress didn't act to disapprove the bill by a certain time frame (the date eventually decided on was September 17, 2015), it would stand. This gave the members the option of a "pocket" approval, in which nobody had to go on the record with a vote at all. Alternatively, the Republicans could force a vote to register their opposition. Even if the nays outnumbered the yeas, the president could then veto to preserve the deal. It was a brilliant solution for everyone, and on May 7, the review bill passed by 98–1. Tom Cotton was the lone holdout.

◇◇◇◇◇◇◇◇◇◇◇

Persistence, so critical to effective diplomacy, is a quality that many women have developed instinctively as they combine work and what we call life. "Nevertheless, she persisted," has become a rallying cry for women since Senator Mitch McConnell used the phrase to explain his scolding of Massachusetts senator Elizabeth Warren after she read critical comments on attorney general nominee Jeff Sessions on the Senate floor. It is nothing new for women to have to persist if they want to do their jobs, or to rise to a position they have set as a goal.

Margo Morris, whom I've worked with for twenty-five years, went to work at the Philadelphia National Bank as a secretary right out of high school. After visiting her best friend, who had moved to Washington to first become a nanny (and later an X-ray technician), Margo decided that she wanted to move there as well. She noticed in a *Philadelphia Inquirer* ad that the US Department of State was recruiting office management specialists—government speak for secretaries. She applied and was hired but had to wait through the five months of security clearance before she could come on board. Finally, she got a call to come to DC. When I asked Margo, who has been my right hand since I came to State, what gave her the courage to take this leap, she didn't know exactly. The only connection she had to foreign affairs, she said, was a Norwegian cousin who was a steward on a cruise ship. Margo had always admired her cousin's adventurism. In high school, Margo had loved to go to a restaurant at the Philadelphia airport and watch planes take off and land. She'd always watch the outbound flights go out of sight and imagine that she was headed out herself.

When Margo began her State Department career, she was only nineteen and thus, under the rules at the time, could only serve in the United States, so she was assigned to the personnel department. When she finally turned twenty-one, she was assigned to London. There she met her husband, a Brit. At that time, female staff were not allowed to be married and serve abroad, so Margo had to resign from State; she was reinstated only years later, after the marriage ban had been discarded.

After a year back in DC, Margo, now with two little daughters, was assigned to Ethiopia, and her husband followed her. Since their time there was during the revolution, Ethiopia was quite a hair-raising adventure. Next on the agenda was Thailand, after which the couple reversed roles and Margo followed her husband for his job with another international US agency. In every move, Margo, talented and personable, found jobs with State: in Kenya and South Africa, and again in Washington, where she and I connected.

When I interviewed her to be my assistant, I saw that Margo was poised, with a welcoming face and manner, and that she was well spoken but serious—maybe too serious. Noting the demands of the job, I wondered aloud during her interview if she ever laughed. She let out one of the most glorious laughs I've ever heard, and in that moment I knew she was the one. We've been joined at the professional hip ever since.

Margo's story has had many more unexpected twists than mine as rules changed for women over the years. When interns come into our office, or when young staffers ask how I got to do what I do, I tell them to spend some time with Margo. She is the real adventurer. She launched her unexpected life with fewer advantages than I had at my disposal. I am exceedingly lucky that she has been my work partner for all these many years as we continued our tenacious diplomatic lives.

Tenaciousness and persistence are required of women who want to work while also covering home. The choices that have faced Kamala Lakhdhir, my chief of staff for all four years I was undersecretary of state for political affairs, are familiar to many women I know. A career

Foreign Service officer (and now ambassador to Malaysia), Kamala managed everything I could not get to, and did it as if it were me, only better. She helped me get to fifty-four countries during my tenure, all while the Iran negotiations were ongoing. Kamala accomplished all this while helping her parents in Connecticut deal with several health crises. Recently, a female CEO of a major pharmaceutical company suggested that we should stop talking about work-life balance and begin talking about work-life integration. Kamala is Exhibit One demonstrating the truth of this. How she has achieved work-life integration may lie in the mantra that underscores everything she does, including the terrific recruiting she did for the staff assignments in the office. "It's all about the people" she always opines.

Having a life that, like Margo's and Kamala's, integrates the personal and the professional is not easy or seamless. Women who work, in and out of the home, have learned to do this out of necessity. So much more has become possible for women in the past three or four decades, though much more accommodation of women—and of all parents—in America is still required. Through this period of intensive change, women have had to improvise, experiment, teach, and outright protest in order to be able to work—all while also handling most of the caretaking responsibilities for our children and elders. Women of my generation, therefore, could rarely plan our lives or our careers. We moved through each day, each job, and each phase of our career by taking the jobs that were offered by employers who were willing to put respect for our abilities ahead of the risk that we'd need to manage another life at a vulnerable time along with our own.

We can all use persistence, of course, for reasons that have nothing to do with gender discrimination. When my brother committed suicide, I was lost for a while, angry and in tremendous pain, but

I kept going and, maybe more importantly, Bruce kept going with me. When his father died, Bruce was left with a hole in his heart that I could not fill up, and before he came to terms with it, our relationship was shaken, but we came through. We have sought professional help to work through our losses, giving each other room to heal, and we've generally done what we needed to ensure that we wouldn't lose each other as well.

It has taken terrific amounts of persistence to stick with a career in an area of government that can be forbidding for a wife and mother. I'm lucky that for most of his career my journalist husband has been able to be at home on a regular basis and be there for our daughter, which has made it possible for me to stay at work. It was Bruce who took Sarah to the emergency room for a broken wrist on the playground while I was in a White House meeting. Today I would be freer to leave the meeting, but such were norms at the time that I thought, particularly as a woman, I had to stay. Needless to say, women in many workplaces have neither the support nor the resources I have had.

Every place I have ever worked has been adorned with two very early drawings by Sarah. One is a primitive drawing of a mom heading to her car and her daughter carrying the mom's briefcase. The caption reads, "Please wake me when you get home. I am a little sad." As grateful as I am for Bruce and his steady support, it's been hard at times to stay at my desk with that reminder there. I've had to push through when it told me that I should be home. The other drawing is there to counter my guilt. It gives me license to keep working on behalf of peace and justice. It shows children playing ball and reads, "When you play together with others, you can have the best time."

◇◇◇◇◇◇◇◇◇◇

As someone who, as I said in the last chapter, has always preferred building institutions to maintaining them, persistence has always been a bit of a struggle. While I preach the value of persistence, I'm the first to say that political campaigns have been among my happiest times—win or lose, they have a beginning, a middle, and an end. If you can only hang in until election day, lose a little sleep, and survive some tense moments, the job is done.

In government, particularly in national security and foreign policy, there is no finality, good or bad. Peace achieved in one year may be superseded by war in the next. New threats emerge—cyber, war in outer space, climate change, terrorism—while the old ones morph from instability to hostility, from Arab Spring to Arab Winter. But the need to scramble our way through crises keeps my cattle-drive juices flowing.

Building a business is hard as well, requiring equal measures of persistence and luck. I've learned over time that after one leaves government service, it usually takes a good year to plant your feet firmly in the ground of a new venture. These transitions always create a level of anxious uncertainty, but I've learned to get through them.

For most of 2001, after the end of the Clinton administration, I worked on a consulting project for Citigroup focused on translating social responsibility to the investment world. During this transition year, I also consulted with my old friend, and now former secretary of state, Madeleine Albright as she thought through what to do next in her life. I looked at a number of options for her, including starting her own foundation or public policy center. In discussions with some fellow Clinton administration veterans—former Environmental Protection Agency chief Carol Browner; Albright's former deputy chief of staff Suzy George; and Jim O'Brien, her former senior adviser and principal deputy director of policy planning—we became increasingly intrigued with the possibility of starting our own international business consulting firm. We also knew that other than Carla Hills, the former Bush trade negotiator, there were virtually no women leading such firms. We wanted to change that.

None of us had ever started a business, and truth be told, our motivations were less about profits initially than extending the lessons we'd learned in public service. We saw global business investment as a force that could build the middle class in countries that had never enjoyed the benefits of one. Long-term, we knew, a middle class pushes for more democracy, more inclusion, and less corruption. And importantly, a vibrant middle class creates consumers for American products, creating American jobs.

The next thing we knew, we were on our way. Suzy George, a lawyer and a whiz at getting just about anything done, set up the nuts and bolts of the business. Madeleine helped finance us at the start, with the understanding that the rest of us would repay her investment as we became self-sustaining. All of us began hustling for clients. The new firm was an adventure, and we applauded ourselves for having the courage to take on something new and unexpected and to reckon with the challenges. Even with the former secretary of state at the helm, we knew we didn't have access to the Washington "ole boys" who give business to each other. That kind of network simply did not—and still does not—exist for women.

In a staggering moment of fate, however, we moved into our offices on McPherson Square, just two blocks from the White House, during the week of September 11, 2001. We'd hardly had time to sit down at our new desks when we saw smoke from the direction of the Pentagon. People called and told us that planes had flown into the World Trade Center towers in New York City. We didn't have a TV yet to watch the news. Finally, someone ran upstairs to former senator Bob Dole's office a couple of floors above us and borrowed one. Like everyone, we were horrified. We watched out our windows as DC quickly gridlocked, workers trying to drive in all directions to get out of the city, fearful of what might happen next and wanting to reach their families to take in the tragedy together.

We also realized that planes everywhere were stopped. All US airports were immediately shut down, and no international business travel was going to happen anytime soon. Meetings we had scheduled to launch our company were postponed. Life as we knew it came to an abrupt halt.

We all eventually got to our homes and sat glued to our television sets. We mourned the Americans who died, the families who suffered, and the new chapter in our country's history. My daughter was a freshman in college, and my husband and I called her, understanding that she would now be forever part of the 9/11 generation. I tried to reach my sister, who worked at New York University, to make sure she was safe. Cell phones were jammed, and even landlines were blocked. But we all eventually did talk and cry together. It was enough that day—and for much of the week—to grab hold of one another and grieve.

In the back of my mind, however, I tried to sort out what lay ahead for our new firm. It somehow seemed impossible that an international consulting business could get under way amid this world chaos. No one was moving anywhere. With the entire world preoccupied with the crisis for our country, building a business seemed a pedestrian concern at best.

But like the rest of the country, we saw that we had to get up and do something. We had bills to pay and our own families to support.

We had to shake off the fear to defeat those who attacked us. Somehow it felt as if we had to do it for those who had died. Moving forward was the only option.

So tentative were those first few days that it was hard to tell at first how hard to push to land business. We trekked to New Jersey to pitch the pharmaceutical company, Merck, but we couldn't quite figure out how to close the deal. Finally, Jim O'Brien and I offered to provide Merck with some of our product for free: we used a pitch meeting to give them some advice gratis in hopes that they'd see our worth. The day went well, and we boarded the train home, beers all around, hoping that one more conversation would generate our first client.

The next day I called our contact, a terrific woman professional who had championed us to her CEO. She told us that her bosses were ready to sign a contract but had asked for assurances that there were other clients. I assured her that we had a pipeline of clients, without saying whether any had yet signed (they had not). She took me at my word that there would be others, and we were hired.

Ironically, and perhaps a bit perversely, those first weeks after the tragedy at the World Trade Center, in Pennsylvania, and at the Pentagon made our potential clients understand more deeply that they needed to understand the world and navigate governments, often in new and different ways from how they'd approached governments in the past.

In the weeks and months ahead, we gradually added more clients until we had a book of business. Over the next fifteen years, our partners moved in and out of government, and we merged with Stonebridge International to become Albright Stonebridge Group, but the core that began the business is still pushing forward together, now having serviced clients in more than 110 countries.

chapter seven

SUCCESS

W hen we finally reached the end, it was as if we'd never got past the beginning. History will record that I spent the last minutes of the Iran talks waiting quietly in a small hotel meeting room, while down the hall the Iranian foreign minister held out for one more compromise, a scrap that would allow them to say that they had fought for every advantage.

Monday, July 13, was day 26 at the Coburg. In the early evening, the Russians and the leaders of the EU team had come to Secretary Kerry's suite at the Coburg to talk through the few remaining issues. Officially, Kerry was staying at the Imperial Hotel, but he was still in pain from his bicycle fall in Geneva six weeks before and had taken a room at the Coburg as a ready retreat where he could go when there were a few free minutes to elevate his leg, undergo physical therapy, or speak securely to the White House without trekking back to his hotel on his crutches. Since he had arrived a few days earlier, this suite had become the hub of the negotiations.

As the Russians and Kerry talked, Javad Zarif appeared, exhausted and wary. A discussion began. By this point, there was nothing really standing in the way of a deal from our point of view. We were only waiting for Zarif to say the deal was done. Whenever we got close to hearing it from him, he seemed to see his life flash before his eyes and set forth on another topic. It soon became clear that he would never be able to come to closure in the crowded room, with other ministers joining as well as all the political directors watching. I suggested that we clear out, ultimately leaving four principals—Kerry, Mogherini, Lavrov, and Zarif—to forge a conclusion.

I stayed close by, in a meeting room down the hall, anticipating that they would get there soon. With me down the corridor were Secretary of Energy Ernie Moniz; my nuclear lead, Jim Timbie; and State's sanctions expert, Chris Backemeyer. All were ready to defray any eleventh-hour technical points. Also on hand were Rob Malley and Secretary Kerry's extremely effective chief of staff and head of policy planning, Jon Finer. Jon and Rob shuttled back and forth down the short hallway as lookouts for any signal that the deal was done.

There had been some last-minute drama, of course. Lavrov goaded Zarif, questioning, not for the first time, whether the Iranian foreign minister had the authority to make a deal, as Kerry, along with Mogherini, tried to get closure in Kerry's suite. Zarif, responded personally, saying he needed more. Then Zarif promptly moved to the door. Using his crutches to block Zarif's path, Kerry urged him to stay. Lavrov, Zarif had to understand, was expressing everyone's frustration. But the moment was useful in crystallizing what we all hoped. Zarif was out of time and out of corners to turn.

Or not quite yet. Suddenly Kerry came hobbling down the hall on his crutches and swung into the meeting room where we were gathered, saying Zarif needed something else, a familiar refrain.

I was out of patience, however, and resisted. The day before,

President Rouhani had tweeted that the deal was sewn up. Though he had quickly deleted his post, he had showed Iran's cards. They couldn't very well kill the deal now.

But I wasn't in the room—Kerry was, and as such, he was a better judge of what was required. In any case, we were prepared for this moment. Chris was holding a short list of people and entities we'd held back that we could add to the sanctions relief. In any negotiation, it's wise to keep in reserve some minor give, so you can appear to yield ground in the end with no real cost. Chris handed a piece of paper to Kerry, who crutched his way back down the hall.

A few minutes later, Kerry reappeared at the doorway and said we were done.

<><><><><><><>

Success doesn't always immediately feel like success. I've found that in the days after a major deal is completed, my body needs a few days to accept what my conscious self knows. My adrenaline, set to "urgent" for so long, slowly drops, and a sort of depression sets in. I deflate.

Besides, getting to yes was only the start of the new process of implementing the deal. The bigger the negotiation, the more work there is to be done when it's over. After twenty-six straight days of exhausting mental exertion and lack of sleep, we still had to put in place strict monitoring and verification measures by the International Atomic Energy Agency before any sanctions could be lifted. We also had to continue working on securing the release of Americans still missing or in jail in Iran, manage the breach with the Israelis and the Saudis, and go home and sell the deal to congress.

And another chore loomed: it was only slowly dawning on me that

I was really leaving State, that I had to train up my replacement, who would be helping to enforce the deal for the remainder of the Obama term and beyond.

Most immediately, we had to read the deal, all 110 pages, to make sure that everything we had agreed to was in the document.

The European Union delegation "held the pen" on the text of the agreement, meaning they had ultimate responsibility for the content of the final document, so their team set themselves up in a Coburg conference room and began reading the agreement line by line. Every delegation joined them by turns in what turned into an all-nighter.

It wasn't until well past dawn on July 14 that the Joint Comprehensive Plan of Action was announced to the press. We sent word to the media to gather not at the Coburg but at the United Nations campus across the Danube. In keeping with UN tradition, all the principals sat around a U-shaped table with their aides behind them. The Iran delegation had its core team on one side, with Zarif at the top next to Mogherini. The rest of the P5+1 was arrayed on the other side in alphabetical order, as had been our practice throughout the negotiation. That put Kerry at the end beside Moniz, who had been given a spot at the table in a nod to his critical role in the negotiation.

The room was small, only large enough for one or two aides as backbenchers, so I sat behind Kerry with only Rob Malley next to me. While we waited for the press to arrive, the Chinese began getting the signatures of all the ministers on their paper copy of the agreement. Soon everyone was circulating their copies to get all the signatures. Since there would be no formal signing ceremony (treaties get signed, political agreements don't), this souvenir was as close as we all got to recording that we were present at the creation of this document.

Finally, the press was brought in, wave after wave, to get photos and video. After they left, the room fell quiet. Mogherini took the moment to invite each minister to make a few remarks about what had been accomplished. We all hung on the words of each speaker as the profound importance of what we had accomplished began sinking in—just as the adrenaline dropped and sleep deprivation started to kick in.

Kerry was last to speak. He read aloud the talking points the team had diligently prepared, but then he let the paper drop to the table and spoke from his heart. He told the assembly how he had gone to Vietnam at twenty-four years old as a young Navy officer and returned to the United States as a protester objecting to the war in which he had fought. He had then made it his life's work to ensure there was never such war again. For him, he said, his voice catching and trembling, this agreement was about that: no more war. The room was completely silent, the sense of history like a weight on us. Then, with tears in many of our eyes, we all began to applaud, even the Iranians.

We emerged from our emotional session to answer questions from reporters. We got word that the president was going to address the nation from the White House, despite the early hour—it was 7:00 a.m. in Washington. Out of deference to the president, Kerry delayed his part of the press conference until Obama had spoken from the White House. We located a tablet and watched President Obama, with Vice President Joe Biden standing beside him, lay out once again the rationale for finding a peaceful way forward with our old nemesis. As I stood beside Kerry, who was looking over his remarks before going up onstage, Zarif came to shake his hand. It was a moment like the one two years before at the United Nations General Assembly that had caused a sensation. Now we hardly thought twice.

The White House informed us that it had organized briefings with reporters and columnists back in the United States and that we all had lists of members of Congress to call, to begin laying the groundwork for the big battle ahead for the congressional review. So once the press in Vienna was sated, we headed back across the river to Kerry's suite at the Imperial Hotel to make calls. We'd now been up for thirty-six hours, and we still had to get to the airport to board the plane home.

The Air Force plane used by Secretary Kerry, a modified Boeing 757 with quarters and office space for the secretary and crew, seats only forty or so additional people. Kerry had opened as many seats as he could for members of the team. We all felt a need to be together, even knowing that we expected to be asleep immediately after takeoff.

Not long after we were in the air, Ernie Moniz surprised us with a bottle of wine. A few days before, he'd disappeared from Vienna for one day to fly to Lisbon to accept a knighthood, in honor of his Portuguese origins—his parents had been born and raised in the Azores. Along with the knighthood, he'd received a very special bottle of Madeira, which he now went up and down the aisle of the plane pouring into plastic cups. Kerry came out of his private stateroom, where he'd been making calls, to join us in the main cabin for a toast. It was a quiet recognition of our hard-won success, particularly compared to the celebration that had already begun in Tehran at that hour. After we landed, we saw that Iranians had come out on the streets to honk their horns and cheer the agreement. People hanging out their windows shouted back. At the airport, a happy crowd was assembling to greet Zarif as his plane arrived. Our celebration was a few sips of Ernie's Madeira before we all passed out until the plane landed in Andrews Air Force Base back in Maryland. I'd never slept so hard in my life.

◇◇◇◇◇◇◇◇◇◇◇

There are different kinds of success, and you measure each differently. Electoral politics has given me some of the most delirious moments of success I've ever known. The night Barbara Mikulski became the first Democratic woman to be elected to the US Senate in her own right was a rush of unadulterated happiness, outranked only by the birth of my daughter three years before and by my marriage to Bruce.

Some years later, when I was working for EMILY's List, I'd gone on recruiting trips to rally women candidates for Congress. In those conversations, I emphasized the hard work of campaigning, of raising funds, and of governing. It's affirming that in most cases this picture actually convinces potential public servants—the good ones anyway. What you don't tell them about is the feeling that comes with winning, an outcome that cannot be guaranteed.

The evening before election day 1986, Mikulski had dinner with a small group of friends and aides at Chiapparelli's, a storied Italian restaurant in Baltimore's Little Italy. This was a tradition she'd started when she ran for city council back in 1971 and then continued through her decade's worth of House campaigns. With so much left to do in the waning hours of the campaign, it felt a little crazy to stop everything for a ritual dinner of pasta and chicken cacciatore. But by this point in any campaign, the candidate needs to be fortified, emotionally and physically, to get through the last long day of appearances and the long evening of waiting for ballots to be counted. And in politics, superstition counts for a lot. Having made Chiapparelli's a tradition in every election for fifteen years, we weren't about to tempt fate.

The next morning, election day, Mikulski went to her polling place to vote, giving the news cameras a thumbs-up, then made the rounds to voting sites to thank her volunteers. In the afternoon, she walked around Reisterstown Road Plaza, a shopping mall just blocks from my father's first real estate office in northwest Baltimore. She shook hands, asking everyone, "Have you voted today?" The opinion polls showing us well ahead seemed to be backed up by the enthusiasm that greeted Barbara wherever she went in the state—even in the rural districts, where the more conservative voters liked Barbara for coming from a modest background and being such a fighter.

Then we waited. Election day is entirely nervous-making, even when the polls say you are likely to win. You pretend to be confident while feeling fatalistic, and you follow every bit of incoming data and every passing rumor. We were so preoccupied with the vote that we hadn't fully prepared for whatever event we'd be holding that evening—hopefully, a victory celebration. We'd reserved a concert venue on the water in Baltimore's Inner Harbor called, aptly, the Power Plant, but with all there was to do to prepare for election day, nobody had thought to decorate for election night, which was shaping up to be a national event. Barbara's win would be the capper on a huge night for the Democrats, who were on the verge of retaking control of the Senate, which had been lost during the Reagan Revolution. Our victory was the closest emblem of that night for the Washington press, and they naturally came out in force.

Fortunately, Sandy Hillman, Mikulski's longtime friend and public affairs wizard, had the presence of mind to order a large red MIKULSKI FOR SENATE banner and get it to the Power Plant to be hung before the results came in. Sandy also turned up dozens of white mums that she used to deck the stage.

I also understood the weight of that night, and while guarding against presupposing a victory (also bad luck), I began to think about what I would wear, as any woman might. Sometime in the week leading up to election day, I found time to sneak out to a small dress shop near our campaign office and pick out something for the victory celebration that was looking more and more probable. The candidate would be in her signature red; I wanted an outfit that would keep me in the background but looking sharp nonetheless. I spent $300—an ungodly sum at the time—on an elegant cobalt blue and black tweed long jacket and below-the-knee black skirt, along with matching jewelry that is still in my jewelry box today. That I can remember with such clarity buying and wearing that outfit is testament to the importance of the evening.

As the polls began to close, the Power Plant was packed, not only with Marylanders but with national political players who had made the hourlong trip from Washington. A riser had been erected at the back of the hall for the array of cameras and the reporters, who were unusually animated, anticipating a historic moment. The energy level was over the top, and I hastily embraced Bruce and my parents before pushing through the crowd to the wing of the stage to ensure that elected officials and family made it onstage as the results filtered in, victory seemingly assured.

After her opponent, Linda Chavez, conceded, Barbara—Senator-Elect Mikulski—went to the podium. Her mother and her two sisters, who had worked beside Barbara in the family grocery in the blue-collar Polish neighborhood a mile or two east of the Power Plant, were already there. Her father was in a nursing home a few miles away. Her brothers-in-law and beloved nieces and nephews were mixed in with volunteers, Maryland movers and shakers, and her mentor and now fellow senator, Paul Sarbanes, all of them ecstatic. As always when she walked into a big group, Mikulski nearly disappeared before she stepped up onto a box that had been placed behind the podium to help her reach the microphone. When she popped into view, the crowd exploded with applause.

Barbara embraced the moment, telling her father, "I know you're watching. Your daughter is now a United States senator!" The crowd couldn't get enough. I could see then that Barbara was looking around for me. She thanked me and brought me onstage for a round of applause and a hug. Never, professionally, had I been prouder. I knew that I'd helped Mikulski win an election with 61 percent of the vote, and I had helped the Democrats achieve a major milestone.

◇◇◇◇◇◇◇◇◇◇◇◇

Success in foreign policy and national security matters rarely feels like this. Campaign victories, like diplomatic agreements, may come after years of dedicated service. As Barbara once quipped, "Mine is a twenty-five-year overnight success." Both elections and international agreements can make history, but history is less kind to diplomatic achievements. They are overrun by events, undermined or declared invalid by succeeding leaders, or simply disregarded. The Iran deal left virtually nothing to chance. The agreement is based on scrupulous inspections and bears severe penalties should Iran violate its terms. But, as we have seen, the world has moved unpredictably challenging the permanence of the Iran deal.

Because success in diplomacy is so vulnerable to changing circumstances, it's important to know before you start what your definition of success is. The Iran deal, for instance, was designed to keep Iran from ever getting a bomb. This definition, set by President Obama, was met, and we resisted attempts to extend the deal's purview to stopping Iran's activities in Syria or Yemen or to bringing down the Iranian regime, as some wish. We were never trying to solve all the problems of the Middle East—only to prevent the exponentially more difficult problem of a nuclear Iran from becoming reality.

There are good reasons for limiting the scope of a deal. If everything is under study, everything is negotiable. If we tried to resolve all of Iran's behavior, in other words, Iran's nuclear program would become just another element to be bartered for other activities we sought to thwart. Better to stop nuclear weapons development in its tracks and deal with other concerns—albeit concerns that include seriously malign behavior—when Iran's biggest leverage had been taken off the table.

Within these narrow parameters, there were things that might have appeared related to the nuclear deal but fell outside our scope. One controversy that hung over the deal and its aftermath was whether or not Iran's Revolutionary Guard had made efforts to build a shortcut to a bomb several years before. As reported in the *New York Times* in April 2012, US intelligence had determined some years before that the Guard had made such efforts and then stopped, but since the issue of a "possible military dimension," or PMD, wasn't pertinent to Iran's capabilities going forward and the United States had already made a judgment, we left it to the IAEA to decide and deal with, not the P5+1. We made sure, however, that the IAEA could use the leverage of the P5+1 talks on nuclear weaponry by negotiating their access to resolve this issue at the same time.

Avoiding "agreement creep" was why I had my team write an entire agreement before we even began to negotiate in earnest with Iran. I knew we would never get all of this ideal agreement, but I wanted to know precisely what the dimensions of our ideal agreement would be. That way I would know when we'd strayed too far toward accommodating Iran and too far away from our initial goal. As it happened, we far exceeded the minimum definition of success set out for us by the president.

It may seem obvious to say that any definition of success should exclude things that aren't attainable. Would it have been best if we could have prevented Iran from continuing to enrich any uranium at all? Yes, of course. But the time for stopping Iran from learning to enrich uranium was long past. Iranian scientists had mastered the techniques for producing highly enriched uranium and you couldn't get them to unlearn it. Gaining the means to rigorously verify and monitor a small civil nuclear program was more advantageous than to try to bomb away facilities they could, and inevitably would, re-create in secret and underground.

Your definition of success must also take into account what will happen the day after you've won. Would it be preferable if the current system of government were to be deposed? Perhaps if a true democratic system was put in its place. We succeeded in ridding Iraq's government of Saddam's Baathists and in ridding Libya of Qaddafi, only to find that there were no institutions behind these dictators. What we learned in Iraq and Libya is that there is a day after the regime changes.

Lastly, any definition of success must be something you can sell. When we got back to Washington, we had just sixty days—until September 17—to make our case to Congress. Knowing our definition of success was crucial in getting the deal through Congress.

◇◇◇◇◇◇◇◇◇◇

Most of the members on the Republican side of the aisle had announced their opposition before they had a copy of the deal in their hands, let alone had read it. Democrats generally supported the deal and the president.

Our strategy was to focus on the votes we needed in the Senate. According to the Corker-Cardin legislation that had ordered the review process, the question before Congress was whether the agreement should be *dis*approved; a defeat for the bill in either of the two chambers, therefore, would let the Iran agreement go forward. The large Republican majority in the House made it a lost cause there, but if we could get thirty-four Senate votes, the president would at least be able to veto any vote to disapprove the deal. If we could hold forty-one of forty-six Democratic and independent senators, the Democrats could filibuster and send disapproval to defeat.

Between the virulent opposition on the right and wholesale agreement on the left was a wide gamut of opinions. The libertarian senator Rand Paul was a "no" vote on the final deal, but he wanted to keep the interim deal in place. Some Democratic senators, like Delaware's Chris Coons, would only commit to the agreement being "the least bad option" for stopping Iran's nuclear push. Others, like Cory Booker of New Jersey, wanted to support the president but felt great pressure from their Jewish constituents to oppose the deal. Nevertheless, those among them who might be running for president one day didn't want to have a "no" vote on their record.

While we looked to the Senate for insurance, we wanted to convince as many members as we could. A veto would ensure that the deal would go forward, but that wasn't how we wanted it to go—in "the weakest, most pitiful way possible," in the words of one Democratic congressman. Even if we lost the House, we wanted the best showing we could get.

We spent August on the phone, talking with members, seeing them in their home states, or meeting one-on-one with those who were in Washington at one time or another during recess. When Congress got back from its August recess after Labor Day, Kerry led the assault on Capitol Hill, with energy secretary Ernie Moniz as his partner. Moniz was incredibly popular with the congresspeople, who saw him as a scientist who could explain the technical aspects of the deal dispassionately—and in plain English. The senators liked Kerry and trusted him because he had been one of them, but Ernie was newer on the scene and was seen as the scientist that he was.

We all made hundreds of calls and paid dozens of visits to Congress, met with think tanks and NGOs, and spoke to reporters in an all-out strategic push directed by the White House, which set up a "peace room." Chad Kreikemeier, a State Department legislative affairs aide, moved to the White House, and along with Marie Harf, the press liaison for the US negotiating team, led the effort under the direction of Chief of Staff Denis McDonough and Ben Rhodes, the deputy national security adviser.

Many members of the Senate and the House were reluctant to give up sanctions because they had been so successful in getting Iran to the table. This was why Senator Rand Paul liked the interim deal; it kept the sanctions intact.

We tried to explain to these opponents that the sanctions were a tool, and not even our most effective one. Sanctions won't ever stop a misbehaving country from pursuing nukes or threatening its people, and they won't force a regime to institute internal reforms. Sanctions only sharpen an external choice. "You can come to the table and get some economic relief," they say, "or you can continue down your path." Most countries eventually decide that the economic hit is not worth it, but they rarely respond to sanctions alone. Sanctions never stopped Iran's nuclear ambitions. As mentioned earlier, at the beginning of European negotiations with Iran more than a decade ago, Iran had about 164 centrifuges. At the time we entered serious negotiations after Rouhani's election, they had 19,000 centrifuges spinning, even though sanctions had been fierce for some time.

At any rate, as we also explained, if Iran didn't keep up its end of the deal, we could snap back our sanctions. This had been one of the last, and most difficult, elements of the negotiation in Geneva: the mechanism by which the multilateral sanctions would be reimposed. If Iran violated the terms of the deal, the P5+1 nations didn't want to have to rely on the cumbersome process of getting a new sanctions resolution through the UN Security Council. The Russians, on the other hand, didn't want an automatic reinstatement of sanctions that would go around the Council and deny them their veto power.

In the end, Russian foreign minister Lavrov helped devise an ingenious solution by which any P5+1 member could demand a vote in the Security Council if it believed that Iran was in violation of the deal. The resolution, however, would be in the affirmative—that is, it would confirm that sanctions relief would continue. Any one country could then veto that resolution, snapping back the sanctions; thus, veto rights were preserved, while the United States or any other country could still act unilaterally.

Once we had this mechanism in place and were satisfied that the sanctions were only suspended, not canceled altogether, we could give some ground on the specific people or companies within Iran or the commercial activity we were sanctioning. The sanctions were not an end in themselves, and we didn't let ourselves get distracted by them, or let our success be measured by them. The United States still maintained an overall embargo, with few exceptions, as well as sanctions for other nefarious Iranian behavior. Indeed, in the delicacy of negotiations, we had used the word "lifted" when discussing sanctions relief, since Iran wanted to use "terminated" and we wanted "suspended." "Lifted" was understood by the United States to be "suspended" until years of compliance brought ultimate termination.

Outside Congress, we focused on friendly groups that were opposed but might be swayed. Because Israeli political leadership had been harshly critical of opening any diplomatic front with Iran, American Jews were deeply divided over the vote, and senators and representatives of both parties with large Jewish constituencies needed convincing. The best we could do was explain why the agreement with Iran was the best, safest option for Israel. I sat in on conference calls to conservative and reform rabbis, though as a Reform Jew, I carried less weight than two devout Orthodox Jews—Jack Lew, Obama's second-term Treasury secretary, and Adam Szubin, who, as head of the Treasury Department's Office of Foreign Assets Control, knew everything about our sanctions regime. Both Jack and Adam are widely respected in the Jewish community. (I was pleased when the *Jerusalem Post* placed me fourth that year on its list of "Most Important Jews in the World"—behind Jack but, maybe as satisfying, ahead of the casino magnate and major Republican donor Sheldon Adelson.)

At the urging of former senator Carl Levin and current congressman Sandy Levin, brothers who served Michigan in Congress together for thirty years and were strong supporters of the deal, Ernie and I flew to Detroit in the company of Michigan's two current senators, Gary Peters and Debbie Stabenow, to meet with key leaders of the Jewish community there and make our pitch. Both Stabenow and Peters showed great courage in ultimately supporting the deal.

In the end, key Jewish members could not find their way to "yes." I talked to Senators Ben Cardin of Maryland and Chuck Schumer of New York as well as Representative Nita Lowey, also of New York. All stayed in the "no" column.

Of these, our biggest fish was Schumer, one of the most stalwart supporters of the Obama administration. Shortly after I returned from Vienna, I had a secure video conference with him over recess while he was in New York, and he impressed me with his detailed, searching questions. (We also held secure video conferences with Condi Rice and Jim Baker and meetings with Henry Kissinger and Steve Hadley, among others.) Toward the end of the review period, Schumer came to a dinner at the State Department with Kerry, Kerry's chief of staff Jon Finer, and me. We answered more questions, but in the end we couldn't get him there. We consoled ourselves that our work might have muted his opposition. He never tried to sway any other senators, and before announcing his own opposition to the deal, he stood aside as the junior senator in the New York delegation, Kirsten Gillibrand, came out in support of it. On the Senate floor after the vote, Schumer said, "Regardless of how one feels about the agreement, fair-minded Americans should acknowledge the president's strong achievements in combating and containing Iran." Under the circumstances, we couldn't have asked for much more.

In the end, we won, on a Democratic filibuster. We had counted our votes well and knew ahead of time that we had the number we needed, giving Secretary Kerry time to arrange a congratulatory reception on the afternoon of September 17. He invited everyone who had worked on the deal across the government to the event, which was held in the beautiful ceremonial rooms of the eighth floor of the State Department. He talked to White House chief of staff Denis McDonough to let him know that we were gathering and would be pleased, his schedule permitting, if the president could stop by.

I was still wrapped up in a meeting in my office on the seventh floor when a staff person came in to let me know that folks were already gathering upstairs—but more importantly, so was the president of the United States. I hurried up in the secretary's private elevator to find the president moving about the room without fanfare or an entourage—Secretary Kerry had not arrived yet either—thanking each person personally for what they had contributed to this landmark agreement. It was a gorgeous fall day, and the doors could be opened to the expansive balcony overlooking Washington. For the second time since that night at the Coburg, I was struck by my proximity to history being made.

The president saw me and quickly said that he and I would have plenty of time to hash over our thoughts about the deal; now he wanted to say thanks to as many people as he could. Soon after I got there, Secretary Kerry arrived, and the celebration continued even after the president had to return to the White House. Every person in the room was touched, honored, and grateful to have been a part of the event.

The day impressed on me the importance of acknowledging our successes. Like many people, maybe even most people, I have a complicated relationship with success. Our fear of failure is well documented (despite the recent vogue, invented in Silicon Valley, for celebrating failure as a prerequisite to success). I believe that we fear success in equal measure because of the expectations that may come from it. We worry that our work will forever be compared to our greatest moments, or that other parts of our lives, our home lives or personal achievements, will pale in comparison.

I am ambivalent about success, too, because it is so often incomplete. Whenever I met with the Iranians, I had a separate bilateral with Majid and Abbas on Americans missing or jailed in Iran. Majid took the lead because of his humanitarian portfolio. Our intense discussions finally led to a completely separate negotiation that resulted in five Americans being released from jail on the day the deal was implemented in 2016. I was utterly happy for them and for their families. But Robert Levinson, a US citizen who disappeared in Iran in 2007, has never been found. Two others, Siamak Namazi and his father Baquer, businessmen with dual US and Iranian citizenship, were arrested after the release of the five had been negotiated. And about a year after the nuclear agreement was completed, another American, Xiyue Wang, a graduate student at Princeton University, was arrested while researching his doctoral thesis in Eurasian history.

For women, embracing success can be especially hard. I often hear myself saying that I "helped" negotiate the Iran deal, or that I "worked on" the most significant nuclear disarmament agreement of recent administrations. I have a hard time owning my absolutely central role in getting this deal—and the intractable Iranians—to yes. (Indeed, I have a hard time writing that sentence even now.) Some of this difficulty comes from having been socialized by the idea that women should be selfless—never ambitious or self-aggrandizing, but humble and subservient. The truth is that no one person's success is theirs alone. Nor is any success under the total control of just one person. Of course, President Obama and Secretary Kerry provided the necessary leadership, Secretary Moniz's expertise was essential, Bill Burns and Jake Sullivan critically opened the door, and the team—the whole P5+1 and the EU team—got the job done. But I rarely hear a man discount his success because he had a team behind him, or say that he "helped" make a deal.

Some of our complicated view of success comes too from what women define as success. We think about success in terms of human relationships. Rarely do I talk with another successful woman about external markers of success—how much money we have made, or our job titles. We talk about whether our work is working for us: Is it fitting into the bigger picture of our lives? Are our kids getting enough of our time? Are we "giving back" enough? How do we find a little time for ourselves?

There is some honor in all this. I always tell young people who come to me for advice about their careers to do what's right for themselves and their families. At the end of their careers, even a career spent in tireless public service, what they'll really have to hold on to will be their family and friends. In the meantime, in the real world of work outside the home, we all have to learn how to embrace and own our successes, how to be proud of what we've done. There's humility even in claiming our successes.

This is true in our personal lives no less than in our careers. Women seem to register success naturally in our celebrations, and sometimes we secretly wish that our partner or spouse would surprise us with a celebration, only to be let down by unrealistic expectations. We somehow believe that the ones we love will know what we want.

Sometimes, though, they do know. When Bruce and I decided to marry, we met my parents for dinner at a fancy restaurant in

Baltimore. As we dined, Bruce pulled out an airplane ticket to Paris—just one, and just for me. When we met, I had been planning a trip to Paris, but in the rush of our romance it had been forgotten. Sending me now was his way of saying that our getting married would never stop me from living my dreams. If I hadn't known before, I knew then that Bruce and I would have a long life together.

I believe that we each must own what we want and speak up loud for the celebrations. In my family life, though we always try hard to step away from our daily rush to get together to celebrate milestone events, competing interests can get in the way. (Heaven knows, I have missed many of these occasions.) We are used to accepting the yearly shuffle of deciding which family will get to see the grandchildren for what holidays, or who will go where for Thanksgiving.

But when I turned fifty, I knew I wanted a special celebration for having made it to fifty great years. I organized a dinner party for myself out at the Old Angler's Inn, a beloved restaurant outside of Washington, invited about twenty people, chose a special menu, and looked forward to the outside setting on a glorious summer evening in June. My family was gathered in our house ready to go when our daughter, Sarah, then a junior in high school, pitched a fit, saying she had finals. The dinner would be too much pressure. She didn't know what to wear.

I took a deep breath. This was my night, but no celebration would be worth it if Sarah was miserable. I sent everyone else on their way and focused on her and her anxieties about getting to the success she wanted in high school. After a few minutes of quiet conversation, we were on our way. When a deer leapt out and nearly sideswiped us as we drove into the country, I did wonder if my dinner was not meant to be. We finally made it, however, and the evening was wonderful, though Sarah was a bit aghast at her somewhat tipsy mother as friends told stories about me. As my husband drove us home that evening, I felt glad and immensely grateful that I'd taken the time to celebrate this milestone in my life with the people I love.

◇◇◇◇◇◇◇◇◇◇

My last week as undersecretary of state for political affairs was spent the same way I had spent my first—in high-level talks at the United Nations General Assembly in New York. Every minister and world leader one could wish to see is in the same place for one short week, and so the days are packed with back-to-back meetings.

Most of my speed dates that last week served to introduce my successor, Ambassador Tom Shannon, to my key counterparts and of course to say my farewells. I knew I would see my European colleagues, and even many of my Chinese and Russian colleagues, at the annual rounds of international confabs and panels on peace and security that I attended as undersecretary and would continue to attend as an alumna of the community. I didn't know, however, if I would ever see my Iranian counterparts again. Toward the end of the week, I went to visit Abbas and Majid in their hotel suite. I had not seen them since Vienna, and now that the deal was done, had passed review by Congress, and was headed for implementation day, we enjoyed a moment of closure that we'd been too busy to have in the summer.

As in the past, we could not hug or shake hands, even in farewell, but the two Iranians had brought gifts of two gorgeous carpets, one from Foreign Minister Zarif and themselves, the other from the Office of the President. It was an awkward exchange, not only because I was not prepared with a gift for them—since we have no formal diplomatic relations with Iran, gift-giving is politically difficult—but also because rugs were clearly more valuable than the sharply prescribed dollar amount the government ethics rules allowed me to accept in gifts. I was still officially on staff, even if only for another week.

I thanked Abbas and Majid but let them know that the carpets would belong to the United States government. I took photos of the carpets just to ensure that I'd have a keepsake, whatever happened. The carpets were cleared by the Office of Foreign Assets Control, however, and months later, after being priced by the government, I bought them. They are now in my office to remind me every day of the essential humanity of diplomatic efforts.

◇◇◇◇◇◇◇◇◇◇◇

My very last day as a State Department employee was Friday, October 2, 2015, the last day of the high-level General Assembly week. The next day, Saturday, I would at last begin my now-shortened fellowship at Harvard's Kennedy School. Early Monday morning, before I had time to settle in, I flew straight back to DC for one last engagement. President Obama had invited me to lunch, just the two of us, in his private dining room at the White House.

It was odd to get a temporary pass into the West Wing after years of access. I presented myself in the lobby outside of the Oval Office and was waiting to be admitted when National Security Adviser Susan Rice and her chief of staff, Suzy George, appeared. "We just want to tell you one thing ahead of time," Rice said. "The president is going to give you the National Security Medal." The medal, a decoration established about the time President Truman created the CIA, had historically been awarded for distinguished service in the intelligence field, mostly to retired directors of the CIA or the National Security Agency (also to J. Edgar Hoover).

Three days before, President Obama had amended the executive order to include anyone who had made an outstanding contribution to the security of the United States so that he could give it to me. "We wanted to tell you ahead of time because we know you'd be emotional," said Susan Rice, "and when you become emotional, you cry."

I was stunned, but very grateful for the heads-up. A few minutes later, we made our way into the Oval Office, where the president greeted me. Susan stood with me while a military aide read out the citation for the medal, and the White House photographer snapped photos as the president presented the medal. I was deeply honored and may have trembled a little as he presented the medal, but I didn't shed a single tear. When the ceremony was over, with my dignity intact, the president and I went to his private dining room and had lunch.

The power of the presidency is awesome. People on their way to visit the president in the Oval Office have been known to rehearse the direct and sometimes tough things they want to say to a president. Invariably, when they enter the Oval, awe takes over and a more civilized discussion ensues. As I contemplated lunch with a president I so deeply respected, I too rehearsed in my head what I wanted to say and how I would balance the intimacy of a one-on-one luncheon with the awe I have of the office.

But the president put me at ease. Over a lunch of grilled chicken and vegetables, our conversation flowed easily. Most of that conversation with Obama was retrospective, as befitted my departure from government. It was not, as you'd expect, mostly about the Iran deal. We spent virtually the entire lunch talking about Syria.

President Obama had been in rooms where I'd been called on to air my views on Syria before, and he knew that I didn't agree with his reluctance to get more deeply involved in the civil war raging there. On this topic, we defined success differently. I had always advocated for arming the opposition, earlier and more robustly. I was interested in pursuing other kinds of actions that would have put pressure on the Russians to get the Syrians to negotiate a long-term solution—such as bombing hard Syrian military targets, not just the ISIS fighters we had fired on, and not bombing empty airfields, as the Trump administration chose to do.

One of the problems had always been finding a basis for these stronger actions under international law. We were justified in our attacks on ISIS because Iraq had asked us to protect its border. A sovereign nation had asked us, in other words, to prevent terrorists from coming into their country. But taking direct action against Assad was, for the lawyers, more problematic. There is no easy US law that allows us to give live-fire support to a foreign group of fighters within another country's borders if we are not at war with that country, though there are concepts of "collective self-defense" and "a responsibility to protect" citizens when their governments do not. These necessary discussions had foundered on their own complexities; eventually they were parked and never resolved.

I understood the concerns about the legal basis for acting. I had met with the Syrian opposition several times and knew it was fraught with problems. There were strong and powerful people in the opposition, but there was also a lot of infighting. I questioned whether the political and military arms of the opposition were connected to each other. But I felt that putting a stop to the killing that was going on was worth the risk. For me, success meant taking firm steps to curtail Assad and using our power affirmatively on behalf of peace.

The president had made his first mark as a presidential candidate by vowing to avoid "stupid wars" and to extricate our forces from our longest and perhaps least fruitful war, the one we were still fighting in Afghanistan. He didn't think the United States was ready to involve itself in another long-term commitment of our blood and treasure. For Obama, success was not having another major new military commitment on his watch, especially a quagmire from which we could not extricate ourselves.

In that sense, perhaps, Obama had won Syria already—by keeping us, by and large, out of it. But it was precisely the highly qualified and temporary version of success that diplomacy offers, the kind that keeps us working for better answers. As we both walked to the outer office of the Oval, and as I went to leave, President Obama told me that he had not stopped struggling with the right way forward in Syria.

I was flattered that the president thought it was important I know this, but after years of dealing with international affairs and seeking peace, I was more than familiar with his struggle. Wrestling with world issues is indeed an education in humility.

◇◇◇◇◇◇◇◇◇◇◇

Our success, as always in diplomacy, was incomplete, and given the occasion, bittersweet. It was only when the Iran deal was finally implemented early in the following year that I could enjoy a true ending to my four years of work, and then it was pure chance that sweetened the moment for me. Months before, I'd been invited to speak at the Institute for National Security Studies conference in Tel Aviv in January 2016. INSS was run by a heralded retired Israeli general, Amos Yadlin, who had been among the most helpful Israelis as we negotiated the Iran deal. It seemed right that my first foreign trip after leaving government should be to Israel. Besides, I had some things I wanted to say to the 1,500 or so attendees and their countrymen at large about the parameters of the deal and why they should support it. In an exquisite irony, January 16 turned out to be implementation day for the Iran deal. I spent much of my forty-eight hours in Tel Aviv in a rooftop television studio doing interviews about both the implementation of the deal and the return of Americans who had been held captive by the Iranian regime. I had an inkling that implementation day might occur soon, but the timing was a surprise.

In my remarks to the assembled, I not only laid out the rationale for the deal but also spoke of the pain I felt as members of the Jewish community assailed this honest effort to make the world more secure. After the speech, several attendees told me that they had never understood what we had done and thanked me for our work. I couldn't have felt better or more successful than I did just then.

EPILOGUE

A month before President Trump made the perilous decision to withdraw the United States from the Iran nuclear deal, I had a conversation in New York with Javad Zarif, the foreign minister of Iran. Zarif had come to the United States to deliver Iran's narrative about the deal to opinion leaders and to the press and I asked for a private chat. We met in the residence of Iran's UN ambassador.

Though Zarif was calm and focused, I understood his emotional climate well enough to see that, behind his usual smooth delivery, he was thinking hard about Iran's options should Trump withdraw. The United States was only one of six partners to the agreement, but our economic might made our participation crucial. Reimposing our sanctions, especially those barring access to American banks to any company doing business with the Central Bank of Iran, would make the deal an all but empty bargain. The progress Iran had made in garnering foreign investment and trade would likely fizzle.

Zarif wanted me to know Iran was determined to control its future, and he wanted my assessment of what I thought might happen.

It was a question I'd been working on myself for months. Since the White House changed hands, the new administration had been undercutting the deal, proposing mitigating legislation, refusing to issue licenses for the limited investment American companies could make. The president piled on by tweeting his usual invective about the deal, repeating his campaign promise to rip up "the worst deal in history."

Each time the administration tried a new tack, a team of defenders would spring into action, faxing and scanning, phoning and emailing key congress members and appearing in the media trying to limit the damage. Increasingly it seemed our defense of the deal was going to go for naught.

Still, I had to tell Zarif something. The most important thing, I said, was to continue to comply with the terms of the agreement—no uranium enrichment beyond the parameters agreed to, open doors to the international nuclear inspectors and so on.

I next tried to impress on him that dissatisfaction with the deal had equally to do with Iran's malign activities in Syria, Lebanon, Iraq and Yemen—activities that Democrats and Republicans alike saw as destabilizing and dangerous. I acknowledged that the nuclear agreement didn't cover Iran's behavior outside its borders, but the administration was nonetheless making Iran's attempts to disrupt and control the Middle East a phantom term of the deal. I urged Zarif to do what he could to convince his government to lower the rising temperature.

Finally, we had a very direct conversation about the need to bring home Americans who had been detained or were missing in Iran. Zarif, who didn't control those decisions, noted that he could not get authority to negotiate a homecoming with the nuclear deal's fate up in the air.

It was a sad discussion for the two of us, who had fought each other, and even some competing parts of our own governments, to put together a deal that we thought was an enormous step toward peace. Now it seemed the situation was lurching back toward violence. We parted, as was the custom, with a bow and a polite smile, but both of us understood the hard reality that was likely ahead.

◇◇◇◇◇◇◇◇◇◇◇

When the official word came that Trump was pulling out of the deal, I was aboard a ship, docked in Valetta, Malta, the tiny island nation in the Mediterranean. *The New York Times* had invited me to be a lecturer on a cruise around Europe. I had jumped at the chance to momentarily escape the dread I felt as the deadline loomed and the White House prepared to exit the deal. But the television in my cabin got MSNBC, and I couldn't resist watching as the president undid our work and put Iran back on the path to a nuclear weapon.

Almost immediately my phone started blowing up with messages from around the world, expressing dismay and condolences (along, of course, with reporters trolling for quotes). My hosts on board the ship treated me gingerly, expressing their support.

Knowing the announcement was coming didn't make it any easier. I had been down this road before, watching a valuable step toward disarmament with a recalcitrant authoritarian state be undone. Twenty years before, it was the almost complete missile deal I'd helped negotiate with North Korea in the last days of the Clinton administration, scotched by the Bush White House. Today we're finding out how hard it is to move an aspiring nuclear state backward once you let a deal get away.

That evening, as my husband and I walked to dinner in Valletta, my cell phone rang. It was John Kerry. He was thoughtful to call, and we shared our anger and our deep concern for our country, ending the call by encouraging each other to keep up the fight.

You may ask, Why? Why continue to try, to argue and debate and push for peace?

Most immediately, I continue to believe that with more hard but necessary work we will eventually come out the other side of this dangerous decision—even if, in the meantime, the president's decision will mean lives lost, missed opportunities for the United States and a diminished standing in the world.

But if you've followed the arguments of this book, you already know that I consider persistence a core value. I don't stop working because the road has just gotten longer. After decades of working as a negotiator, I reflexively seek common ground with those who oppose me (not least with Republicans who support the deal as our best option) and continue to sell a deal to the doubters (some of whom are in my own party). I'm still a convener and a believer in the team that worked so hard to get it right.

These reasons are not so much why I fight on, but how. The truth is that I keep working for a deal because I still carry my parents' faith that the world can change for the better if you have the courage to keep trying, even when it makes you vulnerable. It would be easier for me and those former members of my team to let history take its course. The numbers are against us. It is easy to make our optimism for a peaceful outcome look naive or rash. The president's tweets alone have brought new meaning to Teddy Roosevelt's definition of the presidency as a bully pulpit.

When my parents put their business on the line in the pursuit of racial justice in Baltimore, they instilled in me the idea that important changes only happen if you are willing to risk something. The deal we had negotiated was only possible because both the United States and Iran came to the table ready to stick our necks out. That's what I believe making a deal is all about.

That seems like a revolutionary idea today. Earlier in this book I proposed that power is used best when it empowers the weaker party to do what's right. Those who oppose the deal see power differently. They don't seem to understand why it should not be used simply to dominate, threaten and intimidate.

I keep fighting to keep the deal together because I still believe it is a good one. None of us who negotiated the JCPOA expected Iran to transform itself overnight. The agreement was always intended to be a first step. The Iranian people seemed to understand it this way, as reason for hope. When the regime failed to take advantage of the lifting of sanctions to improve the average person's's lot, Iranians protested in the streets—leading to the arrest of some 5000 marchers—to express their disappointment.

Our current leaders have not quashed this hope, even among those of us professionals whose jobs it has been to leaven optimism with political realism. These days I meet up with my former counterparts mostly at conferences of scientists and political types on nuclear non-proliferation, or on the Iran deal in particular.

One of these gatherings was in Moscow, early in 2017, just after President Trump had only begrudgingly left the deal intact, decertifying the deal but not reimposing sanctions, the first time it came up for his review. I joined a panel with Helga Schmid, Sergey Ryabkov, and Abbas Araghchi as well as Cornel Feruta, an official with the International Atomic Energy Agency, which manages the detailed monitoring and verification of Iran's civil nuclear activity.

I was hesitant to go to Russia, given the evidence of meddling in our election and the ongoing investigations, but it felt like an important opportunity to reaffirm the importance of the Iran deal just as doubters at home were making the loudest noise. The organizers of the conference also told me that the North Koreans would be attending. Ironic as it was to see them at a non-proliferation meeting at a time when Pyongyang was rattling the world with their missile launches and nuclear tests, I thought it might be helpful to hear what the North Koreans had to say.

During my few days in Moscow, I took time to meet separately with my former counterparts. My conversation with Ryabkov was the first of these meetings and perhaps the hardest, given the deteriorating relations between Washington and the Kremlin. I told Sergey that all Americans, Democrat, Republican or Independent, were all furious at what had happened during our election. I expected no real response from him, and got none, but I needed him to know my own fury. We went on to talk about Iran and North Korea, the Mideast in ways we had in the past, loyal to our national views but searching, as is our habit, for any common ground; at this moment, without much success.

Abbas and I met over drinks—water for me and green tea for him. I had admonitions for him as well, telling him that any major efforts by the Iranian Revolutionary Guard Corps or other nefarious actions would make the preservation of the JCPOA even more difficult. I acknowledged that the Foreign Ministry did not control the IRGC, but I pressed nonetheless.

For his part, Abbas asserted that the US president had made his ministry's job harder, diluting whatever influence it had. By shaking the world's faith in the deal, Trump had silenced the reformers and handed a victory to the hardliners who had dismissed the diplomatic foray as bowing to the West. Many of Iran's conservatives were arguing that North Korea was in a better position than them. Abbas and I pressed our points back and forth, both trying to find ways to ensure the durability of what had been accomplished.

The longer we talked, the more we sounded like old warhorses reliving our former battles. Eventually talk turned to our grandchildren, and Javad's as well, and the health issues of those in whose company we had spent so many long hours. I was reminded what extraordinary professionals these lifelong diplomats are. Even as we disagree, and with Sergey and Abbas I disagreed profoundly, we were able to treat each other with humanity and respect.

Later, as we all sat on stage taking turns answering questions from the audience, exchanging meaningful looks as we told our story, I was conscious that these people were my colleagues, in the broadest sense of the term. We'd shared a common goal, even as each of us roundly and fiercely defended our country's national interests. However, the strategic value of building on this common ground was profoundly diminished when Trump reneged on the deal.

In their answers, they handled well the difficult politics of my situation, as an American defending the deal shortly after the US president's first decision to decertify it. I know that some of the reason I keep fighting is that I owe it in some measure to those who I worked with so hard and who risked their own careers and reputations to make it happen.

On the last night of the Moscow conference, I headed for a quiet upstairs table at Café Pushkin, where I met Helga Schmid, with whom I feel nearly as close as I do with any longtime American friend. With a partial view of Red Square, we lingered over borscht, salmon, mushroom canapes, plotting common cause wherever we could—Helga is still in government, but I'm now on the outside looking in. I got an update on her family, and she saw photos of my grandsons. The next day we flew back West together, parting in Munich with promises that we'd see each other soon in New York.

I fight on because of moments like this. When I was a young woman in Baltimore, I never expected I would be dining on borscht and salmon in Moscow with my best friend from nuclear talks. There's no question that I keep fighting for the deal because I love this country, which allowed that young person to rise improbably to a position of such responsibility, to wear the mantle of its government.

At the same time, when I was negotiating the JCPOA, I also didn't expect that the greatest challenge to its success would be not violations by Iran but the political machinations of the president of the United States. But it would be a mistake to think that I am bitter or undone by the loops life has thrown me, even as I rage about the decision. Like so many, I may be daunted on a given day, but I get up the next and get back to work.

When younger people come to me for advice, I tell them what I think will help them in the path they've laid out for themselves, but I usually finish with some unorthodox advice that I will leave you with here. I wish them, and you, an unexpected life.

This may sound at first like a curse, not a blessing. My greatest adventures, the deepest experiences, the most meaningful moments of my life were those that were completely unplanned. If the young person is female, I make clear, as I've written earlier in this book, that she must be particularly prepared to improvise. The unexpected is the norm, not the exception, for women.

We should consider the unexpected an opportunity, and not a burden. It jars us into doing our best work. No five-year plan I could have plotted for myself as a social-work grad student would have led eventually to me sitting in the White House situation room, or in a historic hotel in Vienna, across a table from a pack of bristling Iranian nuclear negotiators, or in a stadium of hundreds of thousands cheering a brutal dictator in Pyongyang.

But if we know to expect it, the unexpected often works out. During the negotiations, my Iranian counterparts would occasionally ask how they could be assured that the deal would be durable. Looking at our upcoming presidential election, they asked what would happen if the other party won. My retort was always that the same could be said about their presidential election, their internal politics. The only insurance we have would be to make the details of the deal as durable as possible. The only way to counter the unexpected, I've found, is to do the best work you can do at the time, using whatever power is in your hands in the best possible way.

Even at the writing of this epilogue, I do not know if the Iran deal can survive reinstated US sanctions. And I continue to worry about and do whatever I can to bring home Americans still imprisoned or missing in Iran. Short term political considerations overtook common sense as the president walked away from both the deal and our fellow citizens. Indeed, on so many issues of concern in our lives, short term gratification is all too often mistaken for real, sustainable progress. And leaders, wanting to retain power whatever the cost, chose autocracy over diplomacy; figurative or literal war over peace.

The lessons in this book, in the lives we all live, teach us yet to have courage, to work with others to find common ground, to persist against all odds, to use all that we are, all our power to do good, and to be not faint of heart.

ACKNOWLEDGMENTS

A wise publisher once told me to write a book only if I was really compelled to do so, because writing is a hard thing to do. It took time and the help of my family, friends, colleagues, agent, publisher, editor, and collaborator to not only own that desire but to get the job done; it is indeed hard work but also worthwhile and deeply satisfying work.

I knew when I began that I could not write the full details of the Iran negotiation. It is too soon in history to share all the substantive ins and outs of that difficult negotiation. But I did want to help people understand the process of diplomacy and negotiations and the tough road to success. I also wanted to answer the question of how I found my way to doing this negotiation and so much else that has been the privilege of my life. I understood that all that I am and have given in service is the sum total of all that I have learned along the way, and not alone through any classroom or course. Our personal and professional lives are indeed integrated and woven together.

I also want to acknowledge that these are my memories and recollections. I learned long ago that although facts don't change, perceptions do, and others may have experienced the same events differently. So, too, the opinions and characterizations in this book are mine and do not necessarily represent those of the US government. Indeed, these days, with the current administration, that likely goes without saying.

More specifically, I want to thank Harvard's Kennedy School and the Institute of Politics for giving me the opportunity to lead a study group that formed the basis for this book. Steve Krupin, a former Obama and Kerry speechwriter who spoke at another study group, first encouraged me to turn my work at the Kennedy School into a book. Steve also introduced me to Howard Yoon, my agent, of Ross/Yoon, who spent hours with me, working to conceptualize a way forward. Howard not only introduced me to Lisa Dickey, who was critical in the early stages of proposal writing, but to Paul O'Donnell, who worked tirelessly, staying true to my voice, to help me actually write the book. Paul is a skilled writer, a good man, and a great colleague.

Books can be written but never reach an audience. I am most fortunate to be published by PublicAffairs, a division of Hachette Book Group. I knew as soon as Howard introduced me to founder Peter Osnos, publisher Clive Priddle, publicity director Jaime Leifer, and senior editor Colleen Lawrie, that I had found the right home if they would have me. They all understood immediately what I wanted to do with this book and encouraged me every step of the way. Colleen Lawrie was a real editor, not only providing detailed feedback and meticulous editing, but pushing me to go deeper, provide more clarity, and help readers come away with valuable insights for their own lives, both personal and professional. My thanks, too, to all of the PublicAffairs team for their assistance and support throughout the publishing process, including Melissa Raymond, Sandra Beris, Cindy Buck, Lindsay Fradkoff, Kristine Fazzalaro, and Pete Garceau, among others. Thanks, too, to Ralph Alswang for his photographic skill.

Thanks go as well to early readers of drafts, including Brooke Anderson, Suzy George, and Margo Morris, who offered corrections, suggestions, solidarity, and honest appraisals, all of which I greatly appreciated. I am thankful as well to discussions with Iran negotiation colleagues who offered valuable recollections. An early dinner with former secretary John Kerry, Rob Malley, Jon Finer, and Stephanie Epner, while Kerry worked on his own book, helped confirm facts included in mine. So, too, former deputy secretary of state Bill Burns, consummate diplomat, was always available to provide detail and support, as he always has throughout my national security and foreign policy career.

Of course, none of my public service was a solo act. I thank every team, American and non-American alike, of which I have ever been a part for their extraordinary service. Public servants, diplomats in particular, have been excoriated of late in the United States. It will only be when we feel the wreckage of their absence that we will fully understand how critical diplomats are to our democracy and to our security. I salute them all and thank them for sharing their world and work with me.

At the core of this book are the women who came first—first to be seated in the US Senate, first to become secretary of state, first to be the presidential nominee of a major national party. Barbara Mikulski, Madeleine Albright, and Hillary Clinton are all extraordinary women I have had the privilege and good fortune to work for and with. No one book can do them justice; they are simply amazing. I am deeply grateful for all that I have learned from each of them. Along with Geraldine Ferraro, Nancy Pelosi, Susan Rice, Ellen Malcolm, and Anita Hill, I have been honored to witness the courage of all of these and so many other women leaders. The same can be said for the women who ran their offices, supported their efforts, and led teams that helped the stars light the sky. Indeed, I salute all of the women in this book who shared their stories and their insights with me throughout the years. Special thanks to the ever-present Margo Morris, who is my rock. For twenty-five years Margo and I have been work spouses and part of each other's families. I cherish her professionalism and her person.

Thanks, too, to the many good men who have helped me along the way. As well as those already mentioned, I especially thank former secretary of defense Bill Perry, who taught me much about leadership; Jim O'Brien, who had the courage to start a business with four strong women; Bill Woodward, who as a speechwriter and book writer was always available to tell me the truth; former secretary of state Warren Christopher and Dr. Art Naparstek, both now departed, each the epitome of wisdom; and presidents Bill Clinton and Barack Obama, who, for eight years each, kept America safe, strong, and a democracy.

I thank my colleagues at Albright Stonebridge Group and Harvard's Belfer

Center for Science and International Affairs for their support, their provision of a forum for discussion of critical issues, and their expertise and insight every day. And I thank the University of Maryland School of Social Work for giving me a core set of skills I have used throughout my life. I have always been a social worker, a community organizer; it's just that my caseload and my community have changed along the way.

Through, and after, our professional careers, it is our family and friends who sustain us in life. I thank my friends for putting up with me, my absences, my forgetting special occasions, my need sometimes to put my work first. Those nearest and dearest to me have always offered support, counsel, ideas, and persistent friendship; I am in their debt.

As for my family, words nearly escape me. My parents, Mimi and Mal Sherman, inspired me, taught me hard lessons, loved me unconditionally, even if at times critically, and shared joy and grief and everyday life, the ingredients of a life well lived. My sister, Andrea, a dancer and PhD gerontologist, has the most generous heart of anyone I know. We may have fought over silly stuff as kids, but we are a team as adults, and I rely on her love and support and hope she knows she has mine. Her own family adds to that equation, and I thank them for all their love. And my daughter, Sarah, now a mother herself and a passionate teacher and advocate of immigration rights and law at Boston University Law School, is my sustenance and continuity. Like Andrea, she read an early draft to ensure that I did not embarrass our family needlessly and to give me broader feedback. Sarah has only been encouraging. Every day she now challenges me to be fierce, to live a kind life, which she teaches her children, and to be inclusive in every way possible.

Finally, my love and gratitude to Bruce. Thirty-eight years and counting, you are my partner, my editor, my intellectual better, my booster, my truth-teller, my best friend, the deep and quiet and passionate love of my life. Thank you for urging me to write this book, but more than that, thank you for living our wonderful life together.

INDEX

Ralph Alswang

Ambassador Wendy R. Sherman, best known as the lead negotiator for the United States on the 2015 Iran nuclear deal, had a long career as a child welfare advocate and administrator, a congressional chief-of-staff, and a political campaigner and consultant before joining the State Department in 1993. She was named Counselor to Secretary of State Madeleine Albright and a special adviser to President Clinton on North Korea. In that role, she managed nuclear and missile negotiations with Pyongyang.

In 2011, she became the first woman undersecretary of state for political affairs. Besides pursuing the nuclear agreement with Iran, in this post Ambassador Sherman was responsible for diplomatic relations in every region of the globe and with all international organizations. On her retirement at the conclusion of the Iran negotiations, she became the first person outside the US intelligence community to be awarded the National Security Medal.

With Secretary Albright, Ambassador Sherman cofounded The Albright Group, an international advisory firm based in Washington, DC, now called the Albright Stonebridge Group, a company she now serves as Senior Counselor. She is a member of the Council on Foreign Relations and the Aspen Strategy Group. Ambassador Sherman served on the President's Intelligence Advisory Board, is a senior fellow at Harvard's Belfer Center and is a frequent commentator and analyst for both international and domestic media.

She lives with her husband, Bruce Stokes, in Bethesda, Maryland.

PublicAffairs is a publishing house founded in 1997. It is a tribute to the standards, values, and flair of three persons who have served as mentors to countless reporters, writers, editors, and book people of all kinds, including me.

I. F. STONE, proprietor of *I. F. Stone's Weekly*, combined a commitment to the First Amendment with entrepreneurial zeal and reporting skill and became one of the great independent journalists in American history. At the age of eighty, Izzy published *The Trial of Socrates*, which was a national bestseller. He wrote the book after he taught himself ancient Greek.

BENJAMIN C. BRADLEE was for nearly thirty years the charismatic editorial leader of *The Washington Post*. It was Ben who gave the *Post* the range and courage to pursue such historic issues as Watergate. He supported his reporters with a tenacity that made them fearless and it is no accident that so many became authors of influential, best-selling books.

ROBERT L. BERNSTEIN, the chief executive of Random House for more than a quarter century, guided one of the nation's premier publishing houses. Bob was personally responsible for many books of political dissent and argument that challenged tyranny around the globe. He is also the founder and longtime chair of Human Rights Watch, one of the most respected human rights organizations in the world.

·   ·   ·

For fifty years, the banner of Public Affairs Press was carried by its owner Morris B. Schnapper, who published Gandhi, Nasser, Toynbee, Truman, and about 1,500 other authors. In 1983, Schnapper was described by *The Washington Post* as "a redoubtable gadfly." His legacy will endure in the books to come.

Peter Osnos, *Founder*